Getting to Work on Summer Learning

Recommended Practices for Success, 2nd Ed.

Heather L. Schwartz, Jennifer Sloan McCombs, Catherine H. Augustine, Jennifer T. Leschitz

Commissioned by

Supporting ideas.
Sharing solutions.
Expanding opportunities.

For more information on this publication, visit www.rand.org/t/RR366-1

Library of Congress Cataloging-in-Publication Data is available for this publication.
ISBN: 978-1-9774-0178-6

Published by the RAND Corporation, Santa Monica, Calif.
© Copyright 2018 RAND Corporation
RAND® is a registered trademark.

Front cover image: Hero Images/Getty Images
Back cover images, top: Ariel Skelley/Getty Images, middle/bottom: courtesy Big Thought, Dallas

Support RAND
Make a tax-deductible charitable contribution at
www.rand.org/giving/contribute

www.rand.org

PREFACE

This report updates our 2013 guidance to school district leaders and their partners across the country who are interested in launching summer learning programs or improving established ones. In it, we present recommendations based on our evaluations, conducted between 2011 and 2016, of summer programs in five urban school districts. The Wallace Foundation selected these districts—Boston; Dallas; Duval County, Florida; Pittsburgh; and Rochester, New York—for the National Summer Learning Project (NSLP), a multiyear assessment of the effectiveness of voluntary, district-led summer learning programs offered at no cost to low-income, urban, elementary students. The five districts are among the nation's most advanced in their experience with comprehensive, voluntary summer learning programs.

This is the fifth in a series of reports stemming from the NSLP. The series consists of the following titles:

- *Getting to Work on Summer Learning: Recommended Practices for Success* (Augustine et al., 2013) is the first edition of this report and was based on lessons learned from our detailed formative evaluations of the NSLP district programs only in summer 2011.

- *Ready for Fall? Near-Term Effects of Voluntary Summer Learning Programs on Low-Income Students' Learning Opportunities and Outcomes* (McCombs et al., 2014) looked at how students in this study performed on mathematics, reading, and social-emotional assessments in fall 2013, after one summer of programming.

- *Learning from Summer: Effects of Voluntary Summer Learning Programs on Low-Income Urban Youth* (Augustine et al., 2016) examined student outcomes at four different times: in fall 2013, at the end of the 2013–2014 school year, in fall 2014 after the second summer of programming, and at the end of the 2014–2015 school year.

- *Making Summer Last: Integrating Summer Programming into Core District Priorities and Operations* (Augustine and Thompson, 2017) examined how summer program leaders are integrating their programs into their districts' core priorities and operations as a sustainability strategy.

This study was undertaken by RAND Education and Labor, a division of the RAND Corporation that conducts research on early childhood through postsecondary education programs, workforce development, and programs and policies affecting workers, entrepreneurship, and financial literacy and decision-making. This study was sponsored by The Wallace Foundation, which seeks to support and share effective ideas and practices to improve learning and enrichment for disadvantaged children and the vitality of the arts for everyone. Its current objectives are to improve the quality of schools, primarily by developing and placing effective principals in high-need schools; promoting social and emotional learning in elementary school and out-of-school-time settings; reimagining and expanding learning time during the traditional school day and year as well as during the summer months; expanding access to arts learning; and developing audiences for the arts. For more information and research on these and other related topics, please visit its Knowledge Center at www.wallacefoundation.org.

More information about RAND can be found at www.rand.org. Questions about this report should be directed to Heather Schwartz at heather_schwartz@rand.org, and questions about RAND Education should be directed to educationandlabor@rand.org.

Contents

SUMMARY

This second edition updates guidance first published in *Getting to Work on Summer Learning: Recommended Practices for Success* (Augustine et al., 2013). It is intended for district leaders and their partners across the country who are interested in launching or improving summer learning programs. In this edition, we distill lessons about implementation that we have gleaned from a six-year study of voluntary summer programs in the five urban districts participating in the National Summer Learning Project (NSLP).

This second edition presents the best available guidance on how to develop high-quality summer programs. From summer 2011 through summer 2014, researchers from the RAND Corporation collected more than 1,200 surveys of summer instructors and 10,000 surveys of elementary grade students, conducted 900 interviews, and observed more than 2,000 hours of classroom and enrichment activities. We are confident that these recommendations are based on the most-comprehensive data currently available about voluntary, academic summer programs.

The successful summer programs we observed delivered several sound educational and youth development practices: teachers with content knowledge using rigorous academic curricula, high-quality enrichment experiences, a high level of engagement between adults and students even during transitions and time outside of class, and an emphasis on consistent attendance.

Putting these elements in place required careful planning. Without it, programs suffered from logistical problems and poor instruction. For that reason, our first recommendation as presented at the end of this section is that a summer program director with at least half-time devoted to this work start actively planning the program in January.

Although many school districts offer mandatory summer programs to students at risk of grade retention, fewer districts offer summer learning programs to a broader population of students as a means of stemming summer learning loss and boosting academic performance. To expand summer program opportunities for students in urban districts and create knowledge that would benefit the field, The Wallace Foundation launched the NSLP in

2011, providing support to public school districts and community partners in Boston; Dallas; Duval County, Florida; Pittsburgh; and Rochester, New York. Each of these districts offered a five- or six-week full-day summer program that served students rising from third into fourth grade; most districts served other grade levels as well. The programs all focused on reading, mathematics, and enrichment activities (such as arts, sports, and science exploration).

As part of the overarching project, the RAND Corporation assessed the effectiveness of the five districts' summer programs. We found strong evidence that voluntary summer learning programs can produce short-term gains in mathematics. We also found promising evidence that, after two consecutive summers, students with high attendance (20 or more days per summer) outperformed their peers in mathematics and English language arts (ELA) and displayed stronger social-emotional competencies.

To help these districts strengthen their programs so that they could be tested for their effectiveness, The Wallace Foundation asked RAND to conduct formative evaluations of the programs over two summers (2011 and 2012) so that districts could make successive improvements to their programs before 2013, when RAND launched a randomized controlled trial. The randomized controlled trial involved slightly more than 5,600 students who had applied to attend two consecutive summers (2013 and 2014) of these five districts' programs. The study examined the short- and long-term effects of voluntary summer programs and the characteristics of the programs that were effective. RAND also continued to provide formative feedback to each district during summers 2013 and 2014.

The recommendations in this report are informed by both the student outcome findings and the data we gathered during and after the four years of program implementation. The rest of this section summarizes our main recommendations. More detail is presented in the main body of the report.

RECOMMENDATIONS

Planning

Launching a summer program is akin to starting a new school year, but with less time for planning and execution. A good planning process might be the most important characteristic of a strong program: It reduces logistical problems and increases instructional time for students.

1. Conduct early, robust planning

- **Commit in the fall to having a summer program.** Program leaders who decided on a summer program in the fall and began planning no later than January ran a smoother summer program with less disruption to instruction.

- **Dedicate a director to manage summer program planning who has influence, authority, and committed time.** The quality of summer programs was better when there was a director who had decisionmaking authority, project management experience, and at least half of his or her time reserved for summer program planning and management.

- **Determine which students to target and plan accordingly.** Decide whether the summer program will be open to all grade-appropriate students enrolled in the district or restricted to certain students, such as English language learners or those in high-poverty schools.

- **Consider a cross-departmental planning team.** The district summer programming lead should work with staff from relevant departments, including curriculum, transportation, facilities to host summer sites, human resources for hiring staff, procurement for enrichment partners, information technology for attendance-taking and for use in the summer program, and communications for recruitment materials.

- **Create a calendar that stipulates task deadlines.** Set clear deadlines to anchor planning and use a shared calendar to signal who is required at particular meetings. This promotes efficient use of staff time.

- **Use meeting time wisely.** Hold regular meetings and use the meetings to focus on developing clear procedures and logistics for the summer program.

- **Engage both community-level and site-level staff in the planning process.** Planning worked best when a summer program director in the district central office ran the planning and involved site-level leads in some of the decisionmaking, such as creating site-specific master schedules or conducting site-specific professional development.

2. Plan for both enrichment activities and academics

Enrichment and district partners should jointly plan staff hiring, training, and curriculum and behavior policies. During the planning phase, establish which organization has ultimate responsibility for overseeing the quality of instruction and managing the instructors.

3. Engage in a continuous improvement process

Plan to administer pre- and post-tests, observe instructors, collect staff views about the summer program, and share evaluation data after the summer ends to improve the program over time and to reinforce community stakeholders' commitment to retaining the summer program.

Teacher Selection and Professional Development

According to the research, teaching quality has the largest school-based impact on student outcomes of any factor. Hiring effective teachers and giving them the support they need are critical steps to maximizing student achievement.

1. Recruit and hire the district's most highly effective teachers

- **Advertise attractive program features and encourage promising teachers to apply.** Encourage promising teachers to apply by advertising the benefits that prior summer program teachers have experienced.

- **Hire teachers with relevant content knowledge and grade-level experience.** Prioritize hiring teachers with this experience because in the NSLP they typically had deeper content knowledge and more-varied teaching strategies for the grade level of students they were teaching.

- **If possible, hire based on staff motivation and performance rather than seniority.** Write a summer teacher job description that sets performance expectations for teacher attendance, hours, and engagement with students throughout the day and not just during their class times. Create a selection process that includes principal recommendations and, if feasible, interviews. If relevant, seek hiring exemptions with the local teacher's union to hire teachers based on their performance rather than seniority.

- **Hire experts to support to students with special needs.** Programs that serve a substantial number of English language learners or students with Individualized Education Programs should hire bilingual and special education teachers to help serve those students. The NSLP districts that did so saw student behavior and learning improve.

2. Provide teachers with sufficient professional development prior to the program

- **Familiarize teachers with the summer curriculum and how to teach it.** Provide professional development on the summer curriculum and give the curriculum materials to teachers prior to or at the training. Model curriculum use in the session, so that teachers get hands-on experience prior to the first day of the summer program.

- **Train teachers to avoid common culprits for classroom instruction time loss.** NSLP programs lost between 11 and 28 percent of their intended math and ELA instructional minutes in summer 2014 because of a combination of classes that started late, ended early, or had prolonged disruptions. Explain during training how instructional minutes are typically lost and model activities to help teachers teach "bell to bell."

- **Emphasize that engaging academic work is a part of summer fun.** Highlight during professional development that protecting instructional time is a key way to achieve rather than hinder the goals of the summer program.

- **Train teachers to effectively check for student understanding.** Through modeling, make clear during training that teachers should circulate among all students during their independent practice to ensure each understands the material.

- **Engage all instructional support staff in academic training sessions.** If the summer program includes instructional staff who support lead teachers, those support staff should be involved in the curriculum and classroom management training.

Sufficient Time on Task

Students in the NSLP study who received at least 25 hours of math and 34 hours of language arts instruction in summer performed better on subsequent state exams. Yet intended time for summer instruction is easily lost. Summer program schedules and staff training can be designed to maximize the time allocated for instruction.

1. Operate the program for five to six weeks with three to four hours of academics per day

If possible, operate a program for five to six weeks with 90 or more minutes of math and 120 or more minutes of ELA per day. This length is to allow a typical student who attends 75 percent of program days to obtain the 25 hours of math and 34 hours of ELA instruction that we found was correlated with improved achievement on subsequent state exams.

2. Provide time for transitions in the master schedule

Create a master class schedule that builds in the amount of time it realistically takes for student and staff to get to the class locations so that classes can start and end at the intended time, even if that means lengthening the program day.

3. Schedule academic classes to occur in one continuous block

Avoid scheduling classes to have multiple parts (e.g., a session before and after lunch); multi-part classes typically lost more time than single, continuous class sessions.

4. Minimize the loss of instructional time by attending to summer site logistics

Late ordering of supplies or materials, buses, and meal delivery led to less instructional time. These logistical challenges were common, but they did improve over time.

5. Communicate the importance of maximizing instructional time to site leaders

Communicate to site leaders and to school and enrichment instructors the importance of maximizing instructional time and how instructional minutes are typically lost. Also explain the desired number of instructional hours by subject or activity that site leaders should be targeting.

6. Provide teachers with strategies for maximizing instructional time

Model activities during training or coaching to minimize time loss at the start and end of class, during the afternoon "slump," and during independent practice time.

Student Recruitment and Attendance

The NSLP study revealed that students needed to attend at least 20 days over the course of the summer program to experience academic benefits. In addition to offering enrichment activities, accurate recruitment materials and incentives can help maintain good attendance.

1. Acknowledge that consistent attendance is possible in different types of summer programs

Across the four summers, the two districts with the highest average daily attendance rates had quite different designs. One was structured like the school year and the other was designed like a camp.

2. Develop accurate, timely recruitment materials

Develop recruitment materials that accurately explain both the program requirements and the attractive features of the program. Communicate several times with parents and students before the program starts.

3. Personalize recruitment of students and their families

The most effective recruitment process we observed paired recruitment materials with some personalized recruitment, such as letters from teachers to students encouraging them to sign up.

4. Establish a firm enrollment deadline

Set a date after which a student cannot enroll in the summer program. Having a deadline enables districts and program sites to finalize staff hiring, class schedules, and bus routes in time for an orderly summer program.

5. Establish a clear attendance policy

In summer application and orientation materials, make clear that the district expects students to attend every day of the summer program. Enact a policy that students who miss more than a set number of days might be asked to leave the program.

6. Track the number of initial enrollees who never attend, as well as summer attendees' daily attendance

Track both because this will enable the school district to hire the right number of staff in future summers and to ensure that students attend enough of the program to benefit.

7. If resources allow, provide incentives to parents and students for attendance

Attendance incentives are most effective when provided to both parents and students, but they are costly. Anecdotally, summer program leaders felt that a mix of field trips and weekly prizes for students helped increase attendance.

Academic Curricula and Their Instruction

Summer programs are short and often provide little time for teachers to plan their lessons. To maximize the effectiveness of instruction, teachers should have both high-quality curriculum materials that are matched to student needs and small class sizes.

1. **Engage experts to anchor the program in written curricula that align with school-year standards and student needs**

   - **If purchasing curricula, adapt them to fit student needs and available instructional time.** When purchasing curricula, a district curriculum expert should adapt them—before they are distributed to teachers—to fit the amount of instructional time available in the summer program, align with district school-year standards, and meet the district's student needs.

   - **Curricula developed in-house should be created by district curriculum experts over the course of several months.** If self-developed, a district curriculum expert should start months before the summer program starts so that the curricula are coherent, comprehensive, and align with or extend the school-year curriculum. Teachers should not write their own curricula.

   - **Provide strategies for differentiation in curriculum materials.** Differentiate activities within lesson plans, particularly for independent practice. This allows students who quickly complete tasks to extend their learning and students who struggle to get additional support.

2. **Encourage instructional leaders to observe instruction of the curriculum and provide feedback**

   Encourage site leaders to observe teachers' classes, provide them with feedback, and build in time for teachers to confer with one another about practices. If the site leader lacks instructional expertise, we also recommend encouraging curriculum designers and coaches to observe instruction.

3. **Serve students in small classes or groups**

   Cap class size at 15 students per adult if possible. Small classes allowed teachers to get to know students' needs, establish norms, and launch instruction on the compressed summer schedule.

Enrichment Activities and Their Implementation

All districts featured fun and engaging enrichment activities, such as art, sports, and science exploration, to differentiate their programs from traditional summer school and to attract students and promote attendance. Some good practices characterized the most well-organized and engaging activities we observed in the districts.

1. Select a model for providing enrichment activities

We found that hiring district teachers, contracting directly with enrichment providers, or establishing partnerships with intermediaries all worked well as long as they were implemented by qualified enrichment staff.

2. Ensure that enrichment instructors have strong content knowledge

As with academics, prioritize the content knowledge of enrichment teacher applicants. Those with strong content knowledge more frequently demonstrated and modeled skills, corrected student techniques, and built on student strengths.

3. Train enrichment instructors in behavior management strategies and monitor their implementation

Model behavior management strategies during training and create written rules that align the enrichment and school portions of the day. We observed higher rates of student misbehavior during enrichment than we did during academic classes.

4. Plan lessons to include sequenced activities

Require that enrichment have preplanned and sequenced activities because good enrichment classes included activities that were organized and engaging and allowed the majority of students to actively participate for the duration of the activity.

5. Plan carefully if enrichment is integrated with academics

Not all enrichment activities need or should be linked to academics. But if integrating them, offer specific curriculum guidance and additional training for enrichment teachers.

6. Keep class sizes small

As with academic classes, cap class size at 15 students per adult if possible.

Positive Summer Climate

Positive site climate drives student daily experiences and enjoyment of the program and is correlated with higher student attendance. The quality of staff-to-student interactions was the item most strongly and consistently related to whether students appeared to enjoy the day.

1. Train all staff on the importance of positive adult engagement with students throughout the day—not only in classes

Train staff to interact with students not just during class time but also during transitions, arrival, departure, and mealtimes.

2. Develop a clear, positive message about the summer site culture and ask staff to convey it consistently to students

To promote a coherent culture and consistent application of behavior management techniques, develop an explicit message about the values of the program and how students are to be treated, and train staff on both.

3. Ensure that site leaders observe instructional and noninstructional periods

Convey the expectation that summer site leads should not only routinely observe academic and enrichment activities but also observe transitions and lunch periods to ensure that staff are sending a consistent message about the site's values and behavioral expectations.

4. If resources allow, consider hiring staff to support positive student behavior

To address some student behavior, such as bullying or fighting, consider staff roles, such as social workers or behavior management specialists, to provide one-on-one support to students.

Summer Cost and Funding

The cost per student who attended at least one day of the summer 2014 program ranged from $1,070 to $1,700, with an average of $1,340. Districts can minimize costs—and maximize value from an investment in summer learning—by following these recommendations.

1. Hire staff to achieve desired ratios based on projected daily attendance, not the initial number of enrollees

About one-half of summer program expenditures was for academic and enrichment teacher salaries. Factoring in no-show rates and average daily attendance rates will help districts hire the right number of staff to achieve desired adult-student ratios.

2. Consider cost-efficiencies in the design of the program, but weigh them against potential impacts on program quality

- **Partner with community-based organizations.** These partnerships not only exposed students to enrichment activities they might not otherwise have experienced but also saved costs because enrichment staff typically earned lower wages than district instructors.

- **Reduce the number of summer facilities.** Reducing the number of campuses where the summer program was hosted saved on some campus costs, such as program directors.

- **Centralize planning activities.** It is often less costly for a small centralized team to develop policies and content than to expect each summer site to create its own.

- **Continue the summer program over time.** The up-front costs of developing policies, procedures, and materials for summer programs can stretch over multiple summers.

- **Extend the school-year curricula.** District curriculum designers can use the school-year curricula to develop additional lessons for a five- or six-week summer program.

CHAPTER ONE

Introduction

Summer learning programs are a promising way to narrow the large achievement gap between children of the lowest- and highest-income families. Research shows that during summer, low-income and non-white students academically fall behind their more-affluent and white peers (Augustine et al., 2016; Alexander, Entwisle, and Olson, 2001; Downey, von Hippel, and Broh, 2004; Atteberry and McEachin, 2016). Although many school districts offer mandatory summer programs to students at risk of grade retention, the results of the National Summer Learning Project (NSLP) study show that many more students, including both low-income students and low-achieving ones, can benefit from voluntary summer learning programs (Augustine et al., 2016). This report provides ideas and practices that districts can use to support the development and sustainability of such programs.

In 2011, The Wallace Foundation initiated the NSLP to expand summer opportunities for low-income students and to understand whether and how district-led, voluntary summer learning programs that feature both academic instruction and enrichment opportunities can improve outcomes for these students. The Foundation selected and began funding programs in summer 2011 in five urban districts: Boston; Dallas; Duval County, Florida; Pittsburgh; and Rochester, New York. These districts already offered voluntary summer learning programs to low-income and low-achieving elementary school students and were willing to adopt common programming elements and participate in a randomized controlled trial for two summers. RAND's six-year study of these five districts is the basis of the recommendations and guidance provided in this report.

Overview of National Summer Learning Project Summer Programs

The five school districts' programs we studied had several common characteristics:

This was the first study to test whether voluntary, district-run summer learning programs can improve academic, behavioral, and social and emotional outcomes for low-income, urban youth in both the short and long terms.

- They were offered in urban settings, mainly serving students from low-income families.

- They operated for a full day for five days per week, for at least five and up to six weeks.

- They offered three hours of reading and mathematics instruction each day, taught by certified teachers in class sizes no larger than 15 students per adult.

- They provided approximately three hours each day of enrichment activities such as visual arts, theater, sports, and rock climbing. These were often provided by community-based organizations that partnered with the school districts.

- They provided free transportation and meals for students.

- They were free of charge for families.

The common elements were selected in accordance with existing research and expert guidance. The programs also were designed to remove potential barriers to participation, such as cost and lack of transportation.

Although all the programs shared these common characteristics, each district selected its own English language arts (ELA) and mathematics curriculum that matched its state standards and learning needs of students. Also, districts differed in several operational features (Table 1.1). For instance, the number of sites per program ranged from one (broken into three "houses" sharing the same facility) to ten. The hours of operation varied slightly, and daily schedules differed, with most districts offering academics in the morning and enrichment experiences in the afternoon.

TABLE 1.1

Characteristics of the National Summer Learning Project Districts' Summer
Learning Programs, 2014

Characteristic	Boston	Dallas	Duval	Pittsburgh	Rochester
Name of summer program	Summer Learning Project	Thriving Minds Summer Camp	Super Summer Academy	Summer Dreamers Academy	Rochester Summer Scholars
Leadership structure	District-intermediary partnership	District-intermediary partnership	District	District	District
First summer the program operated	2010	2009	2009[a]	2009	2009[a]
Number of students in the NSLP study	957	2,056	888	656	1,080
Qualified for free or reduced-price lunch (FRPL)	N/A[b]	95%	87%	83%	82%
Lowest-achieving[c]	24%	43%	12%	39%	81%
Summer sites serving students in the study	10	8	8	3	1, organized into 3 "houses"
Duration (days)	25–30 (depending on site)	24	29	25	25
Daily hours	Varied: seven-hour days usually	8:00 a.m.– 4:00 p.m.	8:15 a.m.– 3:45 p.m.	8:30 a.m.– 4:00 p.m.	7:30 a.m.– 3:30 p.m.

SOURCES: Tables 1.1 and 1.2 in Augustine et al., 2016.
[a] In Duval and Rochester, 2011 was the first year the program operated for a full day.
[b] Boston did not collect FRPL data.
[c] *Lowest-achieving* is defined as students scoring at the lowest proficiency level on either the spring 2013 mathematics or reading state tests.

What the National Summer Learning Project Study Found

This was the first study to test whether voluntary, district-run summer learning programs can improve academic, behavioral, and social and emotional outcomes for low-income, urban youth in both the short and long terms. The overall study combined a randomized controlled trial with correlational analysis and implementation research to comprehensively understand voluntary summer learning programs. Randomized controlled trials are the most rigorous method of causal analysis because the lottery-like process of assignment helps ensure that any differences among the groups at the end of the study can be attributed to the program and not to external factors, such as the motivation to apply.

In spring 2013, the five participating school districts invited parents of third-graders to apply for their child to attend two consecutive summers of free, five- or six-week, full-day summer programming. RAND randomly selected a portion of the qualified third-grade applicants to receive an offer to attend the voluntary district summer program in both summer 2013 and summer 2014. These students made up the treatment group; the students who were not offered a space made up the control group. Students who were required to attend a summer program because of poor grades or who were at risk of grade retention were not eligible for the study because they could not be randomized.

To those students not offered a space in the summer program, the school districts provided a list of summer program options in the area, but these options were not necessarily free, and none of them had an academic component. Based on a survey we administered to all students in the study in early fall 2013, 42 percent of the students in the control group indicated they attended at least a few days of a camp during that summer. Of the students in the control group who attended at least some summer programming in 2013, about half said they attended a camp that was a month or longer (Augustine et al, 2016, online appendix Table B.8).

The NSLP study followed the approximately 5,600 students from third to seventh grade. The most recent set of results describe outcomes through fifth grade and are presented in *Learning from Summer* (Augustine et al., 2016).[1] In it, we find strong evidence that voluntary summer learning programs can produce short-term gains in mathematics. Through correlational analysis that controlled for students' prior test scores, we also found that, after two consecutive summers, students with high attendance (20 or more days per summer) outperformed their peers in mathematics and ELA and displayed stronger social and emotional competencies. More specifically, students who received a minimum of 25 hours of mathematics instruction in a summer performed better on the subsequent state math test; those receiving 34 hours of language arts performed better on the subsequent state ELA assessment (Augustine et al., 2016). Our findings demonstrate the

---

[1] The report on outcomes for sixth and seventh grade should be available in 2019.

importance of boosting student attendance in summer programs, which is much lower than during the school year, and minimizing the loss of scheduled class time, as we discuss in this guide.

Our Approach to This Guide

In addition to the outcomes study, we conducted formative implementation evaluations at the end of each of four summers for the NSLP school districts and their partners. We draw on a prodigious amount of implementation data gathered for those annual evaluations and the outcomes study to develop the recommendations we present in this guide. For details about how we collected and analyzed these data, see the online technical appendix. Implementation data included the following:

- **Interviews.** Between summers 2011 and 2014, we conducted about 900 interviews with district leaders, program leaders (including external community partners in two of the five districts), school and site leaders, curriculum coaches, academic teachers, enrichment teachers, leaders of the organizations providing enrichment, and teacher aides. Interviews inform the recommendations made about planning, academic curriculum, and enrichment activities in Chapters Two, Six, and Seven, respectively.

- **Surveys.** In each of the four summers, we invited all academic teachers to take a survey. We also invited all enrichment instructors to take a survey in summers 2011 and 2012. Altogether, we surveyed more than 1,200 summer instructors. During the two summers in which the randomized controlled trial occurred, 93 percent and 99 percent, respectively, of those we invited took the survey. These surveys inform recommendations about planning, teacher training, academic curriculum, and enrichment activities in Chapters Two, Three, Six, and Seven, respectively.

- **Observations.** In each summer, we observed summer sites with successively longer and more-comprehensive observation protocols. In all, we observed more than 2,000 hours of summer program activities. In summers 2013 and 2014, a RAND observer followed each classroom of students for one full day, creating a minute-by-minute time log of the program's mathematics, ELA, and enrichment classes. We added a daily site survey in summer 2014 with questions for the RAND observer to fill out about the climate and organization of the site. The summer 2014 classroom observations and the daily site surveys inform the recommendations about teacher training, time on task, enrichment activities, and summer climate in Chapters Three, Four, Seven, and Eight, respectively.

- **Curriculum review.** In 2011, we engaged two elementary education professors, one for reading and one for mathematics, to examine the quality of the written ELA and mathematics curricula used in all the districts except for one, where teachers developed their own curricula for the summer. The professors did not examine the curricula in this district because each classroom teacher used a different curriculum. In 2012–2014, curriculum experts providing technical assistance to the NSLP initiative reviewed the districts' summer curricula. These reviews inform the academic curriculum discussion in Chapter Six.

- **District data.** After each summer, we collected student attendance records and provided feedback to the districts about how to improve the quality of attendance data. We also collected detailed summer 2014 program expenditure and revenue data. Summer student attendance and cost data inform our recommendations about planning, student recruitment and attendance, and costs in Chapters Two, Five, and Nine, respectively.

Organization of the Guide

The chapters of this guide are organized in the approximate chronological order of planning for a summer learning program and then launching it. Within each chapter, we discuss each recommendation under a separate heading. All of the recommendations found in the chapters are also listed in the Summary at the front of this report.

We organize this guide around the key components of summer learning programs. Chapter Two highlights how to conduct the planning process for summer, a crucial activity to begin early and get right so that other program elements work effectively. Chapter Three recommends practices for the recruitment and training of teachers. Chapter Four describes ways to schedule the program overall and to schedule for the summer program day to minimize the loss of instructional time. Chapter Five describes recruiting students and then tracking their attendance once they are enrolled. Chapters Six and Seven focus on curricula and content for academics and enrichment activities. Chapter Eight discusses positive climate, which is a key determinant of students' daily experience of the program and is correlated with student attendance. Chapter Nine concludes with a discussion of program costs and sources of revenue, with an eye toward sustaining summer programs by limiting costs.

CHAPTER TWO

Planning

Launching a quality summer program is akin to launching the school year, only with less time for planning and execution.

To successfully develop effective and enjoyable programs at scale, program leaders need to identify facilities; hire site leaders and teachers; select enrichment providers; choose summer curricula; train staff; recruit students; actively promote consistent attendance; and manage logistics, such as transportation, meals, and supplies. These are challenging tasks that require months of planning while the school year is in full swing.

In our observations of districts over four summers, we witnessed the benefits of good planning and the problems created by poor planning. To determine what planning practices worked well, we relied on both self-reports from summer program staff and our direct observations of site logistics, and we analyzed our interview and survey data to identify relationships between planning practices and both logistics and time for instruction during the summer program. We found that districts in which the planning process was managed well had fewer logistical problems and spent more time on instruction. Based on these observations, we present the following recommendations on planning.

Conduct Early, Robust Planning

Commit in the Fall to Having a Summer Program

> Program leaders who commit to a summer program in the fall and begin planning no later than January run a smoother summer program with less disruption to instruction.

Program leaders who commit to a summer program in the fall and begin planning no later than January run a smoother summer program with less disruption to instruction. When site leaders in our study districts were hired in January or February, they could participate in district-level planning and conduct their own site-level planning. Planning at both the district and the summer site levels resulted in a smoother program start-up and fewer logistical challenges. When teachers were selected in the winter, they were in place to participate in all trainings leading up to the summer programs. When curriculum selection and pacing guide development began in the winter, teachers had these materials in time for training on the summer curriculum. When enrichment providers were identified in the winter, district boards could approve contracts with sufficient time to pay providers for advance planning, staff hiring, and material purchases.

In those districts where the commitment to or planning for a summer program was made later in the school year, there were too many start-up tasks to achieve in too short a time. For example, late planning led to ordering curriculum materials too late for them to be delivered in time for professional development or even for the summer program itself, causing teachers to scramble and revise lesson plans to accommodate the lack of materials and supplies. Some teachers were hired so late that they missed the pre-program training sessions. Late planning also exacerbated the challenges of transportation route planning, particularly in cases in which districts allowed late enrollments, as we discuss later.

Dedicate a Director to Manage Summer Program Planning Who Has Influence, Authority, and Committed Time

Planning for summer is time-consuming and requires coordination across multiple district departments. We observed higher program quality when there was a district employee who had at least half of her time devoted to planning and launching the summer program. This person, rather than leaders at each individual summer site, made core program design decisions, such as identifying student eligibility for the program, overseeing the process for hiring teachers, arranging for bus transportation, and selecting curricula. Once these key decisions were made centrally, site leaders could then customize them to meet the needs of their sites.

The districts with the smoothest summer program launches over the four years had a summer program director with the following characteristics:

- a job title that specified leading summer planning

- at least half her time protected from other district projects and devoted to managing the summer program

- experience with project management

- sufficient authority and/or influence to work with leaders of the various departments within the district.

Dedicated planning leaders with time could pay attention to details and manage long to-do lists. In the districts in which the summer program planners had the responsibility as an "add-on" to their primary responsibilities, we observed late ordering and delivery of curriculum materials and supplies and late notification of parents regarding acceptances and bus routes.

Lack of strong project management experience led to logistical problems, poorly designed partnerships with enrichment providers, insufficient planning of professional development sessions (for example, trainers were not identified until the day before the training, which led to poor content delivery), and poor guidance to summer site leads. Lack of authority or influence resulted in an inability to get key departments, such as curriculum and transportation, to engage in planning; this resulted in delays because each decision needed to be cleared by a supervisor who did not have regular engagement with the summer lead. Each summer, we observed that at least some of the summer program directors had insufficient time, management skills, or authority.

Determine Which Students to Target and Plan Accordingly

An important early planning task is deciding which students to serve in the summer program (or programs). This decision is made by examining available resources and identifying district priorities. For example, district and program leaders might decide to focus on students at risk of grade retention, those

> We observed higher program quality when there was a district employee who had at least half of her time devoted to planning and launching the summer program.

in high-poverty schools, those with Individualized Education Programs (IEPs), or English language learners. An alternative to targeting specific groups of students for summer programs is to allow any student in the district to enroll based on the principle that summer programs can benefit all students, not just those with specific learning needs or characteristics.

The districts in our study each served a wide range of students in their programs, and, over time, the program leaders better appreciated the implications of this choice. Because the programs we studied were open to students with a broad range of skills and knowledge, program leaders needed to start developing the curriculum in the fall to accommodate heterogeneous skill levels; it takes longer to develop a range of materials to meet a wide variety of students' academic needs than it does to develop a program with a narrower focus. The programs we studied also served students with IEPs. Over time, program leaders learned the importance of providing these students with the same supports they had during the school year, including teachers with special education certifications, as we discuss in greater detail in Chapter Three. This staffing model was more expensive, which had implications for other programmatic decisions.

Consider a Cross-Departmental Planning Team

To find out more: Our 2017 report offers further details on how districts established cross-departmental planning teams and tapped district expertise (Augustine and Thompson, 2017).

To launch a summer program, district leaders are dependent on a multitude of departments, such as curriculum, transportation, human resources, procurement, information technology, and facilities. Engaging these departments in planning for summer while they had pressing school-year responsibilities proved challenging. To mitigate this challenge, two of the study districts created cross-departmental planning teams to engage multiple departments in the planning process. For example, one district that set up an effective planning team included the following job titles in its committee: transportation coordinator, director of student services reforms, technology implementation specialist, food services director, curriculum writer, and human resources coordinator. All the leaders of the district's summer programs, including extended school-year services and credit recovery, were also members of this team.

Summer leaders also sought out additional expertise within the district, such as communications staff who could draft recruiting messages and human resource directors who could write and post staff positions, to create more-effective and more-efficient processes. For example, when the designated summer program leader worked with district budget analysts, she was able to identify more revenue sources for the summer program than she originally planned.

Create a Calendar Stipulating Task Deadlines

Planning summer programs means managing several simultaneously moving activities. In one of the districts we studied, the lead for summer programming created a summer planning and operations calendar detailing what needed to be done and by whom, along with due dates. This calendar was posted on an electronic bulletin board that everyone involved in summer planning could access. It anchored planning in several ways. The timing of planning meetings was contingent on the due dates, and agendas aligned with the tasks on the calendar. Meeting attendees were also dictated by the calendar; the planning lead would invite only the departments relevant to the agenda items. Although we heard complaints in other districts about having to attend meetings about summer planning that were irrelevant or attending meetings in which no one present had the authority to make decisions, we did not hear such complaints in the district that used this calendaring approach.

> **TOOL**
>
> For a sample summer program planning calendar, visit The Wallace Foundation's Summer Learning Toolkit (undated).

Use Meeting Time Wisely

Because planning for summer programming (ideally) takes place during the busy school year, it is even more important to host productive and efficient meetings. We found that effective planning featured regular meetings to develop policies, procedures, and plans, both at the program level and the site level. The summer program suffered in districts that did not hold regular meetings or did not use meeting time productively. In one district, participants met regularly but reported a low return on the time invested. They wished that less time had been spent on trust-building activities and games and more time on developing procedures, such as daily schedules, attendance-taking, material delivery processes, and transportation logistics. Because they did not spend enough time on these topics before the program launched, these logistical arrangements were made hastily, which affected the day-to-day execution of the summer program.

Engage Both Community-Level and Site-Level Staff in the Planning Process

Planning for summer entails making decisions that affect all summer sites equally and making site-specific decisions. Planning appeared to be most effective when an empowered central district (or out-of-school-time intermediary) staff member directed the summer program planning and involved the staff who would lead the summer sites in some of the decisionmaking. In the districts using this approach, planning was comprehensive and dispersed across several individuals, which meant that more could be done in a short amount of time. Site leaders could tailor program implementation to their location (e.g., planning student drop-off and pick-up logistics that worked for the building) while relying on central office district staff for policy guidance and logistical support.

In the districts in which central office staff solely led the planning, site leaders and teachers did not believe they were brought on early enough for site-based planning. Conversely, when site leaders were given full authority to plan a program without centralized decisions from the district, they did not always realize the extent of their responsibilities. For example, one site leader did not know that she needed to get parent permission ahead of time for field trips and had to cancel them at the last minute.

As an example of an effective combination of district-led decisionmaking and site leader input, one district central office staff created templates that site leaders then used to plan, adhering to district-set timelines. Planning-template sections included a sample master schedule for site leaders to adjust; a timeline communicating deadlines for payments, curriculum delivery, and staff hiring; directives about how to communicate bus routes to parents; a template with directions for taking student attendance; a sample student behavior policy for sites to adjust as needed; and a list of program requirements, such as the minimum number of days and hours offered and the schedule for submitting attendance records.

Plan for Both Enrichment Activities and Academics

Enrichment activities can provide students with experiences and opportunities they might not otherwise have, and they can also provide added motivation for students to attend programs. Although all five districts in the NSLP took this approach, the enrichment components of the programs did not always get enough attention in the planning process. For example, enrichment instructors were often hired without a full understanding of the goals of the program. Some quit after they learned that they would be working with large groups of students who did not necessarily have prior training in the teachers' areas of expertise, such as dance or instrumental music. Furthermore, enrichment teachers reported in staff surveys that they lacked information on how to effectively manage student behavior. In each of four summers, RAND observers noted more off-task and poor behavior during enrichment than during the school portion of the day.

However, we did note improvements over time. As enrichment and district partners began to jointly plan staff hiring, training, and curriculum and behavior policies, RAND noted greater continuity for students across the school and enrichment portions of the day. When one or more school-day staff participated in enrichment activities, we also observed more uniformity in program operations across the school and enrichment portions of the day.

An important component of early planning for enrichment is carefully establishing and clearly communicating roles and responsibilities. Especially in arrangements in which community-based organizations (CBOs) hire instructors to lead enrichment in district-led summer programs, intentional preplanning is needed to specify which organization has ultimate responsibility to oversee the quality of instruction and manage the instructors.

Engage in a Continuous Improvement Process

Evaluate the Implementation and the Outcomes of the Summer Program

Summer programs benefit from continuous quality improvement processes, just like other types of academic initiatives. Each summer from 2011 through 2014, RAND observed implementation of the district programs, including their logistics, instructional quality, student attendance, and site climate. RAND also provided data and recommendations back to the districts. This enabled district leaders to get a full picture of different aspects of intended versus actual implementation (some of which they were not

> As enrichment and district partners began to jointly plan staff hiring, training, and curriculum and behavior policies, RAND noted greater continuity for students across the school and enrichment portions of the day.

directly involved in, such as use of classroom time) and to plan for improvements in subsequent summers. RAND studied program outcomes by directly assessing students in the fall; examining their course grades, attendance, spring state assessment scores in mathematics and reading, and scores on a social-emotional assessment; and administering a survey during the summer to teachers on students' social-emotional characteristics.

To make year-on-year improvements to the academic and enrichment programming, we recommend tracking student attendance well, obtaining stakeholder feedback, and conducting observations of instruction. We recommend consulting published evaluations of summer programs for data collection models. For instance, the online appendix for this document provides instruments used in this study. To understand learning outcomes, conducting pre- and post-tests that are aligned with the summer curriculum at the beginning and end of the summer program is a good start and provides an indication of whether students learned what was intended. Comparing the subsequent scores on district or state tests of students who have gone through the summer programs with the scores of demographically similar students who have not is another recommended approach but requires more analytic time and trained staff from the research and evaluation division of the district.

Create a Process for Sharing Evaluation Data with Decisionmakers

Those who invest time, money, and other resources in a summer program should learn about the program's results. Annual in-person meetings of funders, district leaders, enrichment program directors, and site-level summer program leaders were an effective venue for reviewing high-level implementation results in one of the study cities. These results might include data from end-of-summer instructor surveys, pre- and post-tests of students administered during the summer, attendance rates, intended versus actual numbers of students served, and observations of the summer program. Learning what did and did not go well and demonstrating a data-driven continuous improvement process proved an effective way to amass political and financial support, both inside and outside the district, to sustain summer programming.

> To make year-on-year improvements to the academic and enrichment programming, we recommend tracking student attendance well, obtaining stakeholder feedback, and conducting observations of instruction.

Use Evaluation Results to Inform the Next Summer's Planning

Following a continuous quality improvement cycle means using data to make decisions. The districts that made use of the recommendations provided to them as part of a well-planned continuous improvement process substantially improved their programs. For instance, one district adopted a new curriculum based on feedback from the study, and the next summer it moved from having the least time dedicated to academic instruction to having the most. Another, reflecting on site climate data, hired staff to focus on student behavior and thereby greatly reduced the amount of bullying and physical fighting reported in teacher surveys in subsequent summers. In addition, some districts improved the cost-effectiveness of their programs by accounting for the prior summer's no-show rates and, accordingly, hiring fewer staff at the site level. Alternatively, districts could admit additional students to fill slots left by students who signed up but failed to attend.

CHAPTER THREE

Teacher Selection and Professional Development

Curriculum is necessary but not sufficient for high-quality programming; qualified, effective teachers are key.

The quality of teachers has the largest impact of any school feature on student outcomes (Sanders and Rivers, 1996; Wright, Horn, and Sanders, 1997; Sanders and Horn, 1998; Rowan, Correnti, and Miller, 2002; Rivkin, Hanushek, and Kain, 2005). In this chapter, we offer guidance on how to hire effective summer teachers and give them the training they need—critical steps in achieving instructional quality. We base our guidance on both general education research and our evaluations of the summer learning programs, including observations of training and teachers' reports about how well prepared they felt for teaching in the summer program.

Recruit and Hire the District's Most Highly Effective Teachers

Summer presents an opportunity for struggling students to receive additional time to engage with academic material. To maximize their investments in the summer, districts need to hire their best and most highly motivated teachers. We present four recommendations on recruiting and hiring.

Advertise Attractive Program Features and Encourage Promising Teachers to Apply

Because teachers throughout a district might be unfamiliar with what it is like to teach in a summer program, we recommend communicating the benefits when recruiting teachers. When we surveyed teachers after their summer employment, we learned that they were very satisfied with their experiences. In summer 2013, for example, depending on the district, an average of between 81 and 97 percent of teachers agreed that they enjoyed teaching in the summer program. During the following summer, we delved into this result and learned that summer teachers liked having access to new curriculum materials, teaching small classes, teaching only one subject, having supportive site leaders and coaches, and working a half day. Not all summer programs might have each of these features, but to the extent that a program does have them, they should be advertised to prospective teachers.

Some districts encouraged promising teachers to apply. Program leaders used evaluation scores to establish a pool of teachers from which to recruit. Before posting summer teaching positions across the district, they targeted these teachers, who then had the opportunity to apply early. In one district, the superintendent sent an email with the announcement to these teachers asking them to consider teaching in the summer program.

Hire Teachers with Relevant Content Knowledge and Grade-Level Experience

Summer teachers do not have weeks to get to know their students and the curriculum material. By matching teachers' summer experience to their school-year experience, districts aimed to maximize teacher knowledge of grade-level standards and varied teaching strategies that match children's developmental stages, which allowed teachers to begin instruction quickly. Beyond certification and experience in the district, we found that summer teachers who had taught the summer-assigned subject in either the sending or the receiving grade level were more likely to have deep content and content-specific pedagogical knowledge for the grade of students they were teaching. For this reason, districts assigned teachers to grade levels and subjects that matched the teachers' recent experience—avoiding, for instance, assigning a middle-school physical education teacher to teach third-grade reading.

> [We] learned that summer teachers liked having access to new curriculum materials, teaching small classes, teaching only one subject, having supportive site leaders and coaches, and working a half day.

> **TOOL**
>
> For a sample teacher job description that sets performance expectations, visit The Wallace Foundation's Summer Learning Toolkit (undated).

If Possible, Hire Based on Motivation and Performance Rather Than Seniority

To maximize the investment in summer programs, districts desired to hire for summer those teachers who were most effective and motivated. Some of the districts we studied adopted rigorous selection processes for hiring motivated teachers for the summer program. These processes were typically specified in a detailed job description that included expectations for, and benefits of, the position. For example, expectations might be that teachers use no vacation time during the summer program; that teachers engage with students throughout the day, including during meals; and that teachers participate in enrichment activities. The ensuing selection processes consisted of requiring teachers to write an essay explaining their motivation to work in the summer program, conducting interviews with teachers as part of the hiring process, soliciting recommendations from principals, and even observing teachers in the classroom before extending offers.

> [M]atching teachers' summer experience to their school-year experience ... allowed teachers to begin instruction quickly.

We note that many districts are bound by union regulations that dictate how teachers are hired for summer. Often these union agreements require districts to hire by seniority. The NSLP district that adopted the most-selective hiring procedures had to negotiate with its local teachers' union first, as described in Box 3.1. Where possible, we recommend seeking similar hiring exemptions.

BOX 3.1
An Example of Performance-Based Hiring

When initiating the summer program, this district negotiated with the teachers' union to allow a different hiring procedure for the summer program at its lowest-performing schools. The traditional hiring process, by contrast, had two conditions: (1) teachers were not allowed to teach two consecutive years of summer school, and (2) teachers were selected by seniority. The agreement with the union allowed the district to avoid these restrictions and use performance-based hiring for summer programs. For the lowest-performing schools, many principals reported that they actively recruited their "best" teachers, many of whom had taught in the program in prior summers.

Principals, along with district staff, including human resources, reviewed all teacher applications in one day. The team based their selections on principal recommendations and student performance data from statewide tests. Most of the teachers they selected had either taught at a site where the summer program was hosted or at schools whose students attended the summer program site, which made them familiar with the school culture—and, in some cases, even the students they would teach.

Hire Experts to Support Students with Special Needs

Most students' IEPs specify services and support during the school year but not during the summer. The five districts' summer programs served many students who had school-year IEPs that did not specify services during the summer months, and the programs also served many English language learners. Multiple stakeholders responded that it was unfair and unwise to not provide the support that these students needed during the summer.

When we began observing these programs, these supports did not exist in all programs, and both teachers and site leaders feared that these students were not benefiting as much as they could have been. Initially, program leaders had hoped that the small class sizes would negate the need to hire specialized teachers, which increases the cost of a program. Over time, however, they realized that, despite the small class sizes, these students were not getting the specialized support they needed.

Some districts hired bilingual and special education teachers and coaches to assist these students during the summer. Site leaders found these support personnel to be instrumental to students' success. In some programs, these teachers and coaches were originally hired to be with the students only during academic instruction. In these cases, we noted a marked difference in student behavior between the academic and enrichment portions of the day. In subsequent summers, contracts were extended to the full day so that these teachers and coaches could support students during lunch, recess, transition times, and enrichment programming.

Provide Teachers Sufficient Professional Development Prior to the Program

Research indicates that teachers are better able to use a curriculum if they have seen it demonstrated and have time to practice it themselves (Penuel et al., 2007). Many schools regularly provide this type of support during the school year, and summer teachers need such support as well.

Familiarize Teachers with the Summer Curriculum and How to Teach It

The most important objective of teacher training is to familiarize teachers with the summer curriculum and help instruct them in how to teach it. In the district in which the highest proportion of teachers surveyed reported that they felt well prepared, training consisted of three hours on the ELA and three hours on the mathematics curriculum before the summer program began. A large proportion of these teachers had previously taught in the summer program and used the curriculum in a prior summer; these factors also might have contributed to teachers' sense of preparation.

Training was most effective when teachers had the curriculum materials in hand at the training. As one teacher noted in an interview:

> It would be more helpful if they could walk us through the curriculum. . . . If you just give it to us and expect [us] to teach it, it's going to get taught in many different ways. . . . If they show it to us, then we can get a better sense of what/how they want us to teach.

When the curriculum materials were on hand during professional development, teachers reported being more prepared to use the curriculum and were more likely to rate the professional development as useful. However, curriculum materials sometimes arrived after the training had been delivered. In these cases, trainers described the curriculum generally but were not able to refer teachers to relevant sections of their own curriculum materials, which reduced the usefulness of the training.

Curriculum training should focus on practice—how to *implement* the curriculum—and not simply on providing information *about* the curriculum. Curriculum materials often lack specific guidance for teachers. Effective training offers opportunities for teachers and other support staff who will be in the classroom to practice the lessons or activities. In one district, curriculum coaches had teachers work with partners in practicing a lesson during professional development.

In other districts, though, training on the curriculum, particularly when offered right before the start of the summer program, was often crowded out by discussions of logistics. Teachers came to the training wanting to know how many students they would have in their classrooms, what grade levels they would teach, which rooms they were assigned to, etc. In situations such as these, curriculum training was reduced to trainers simply

Curriculum training should focus on practice—how to *implement* the curriculum— and not simply on providing information *about* the curriculum.

handing out the curriculum materials and asking teachers whether they had any questions. In cases in which district leads ordered curriculum materials late, materials were delivered after professional development occurred.

To ensure that sufficient time is spent on training on the curriculum, we recommend that districts offer separate training time to address logistics, or the district could provide this information to teachers prior to the curriculum training. Doing so would enable teachers to better focus on the curriculum training.

Train Teachers to Avoid Common Culprits for Classroom Instruction Time Loss

Even a five-week summer program is a short time period in which to catch up struggling learners or get them ahead for the next year. As we describe in the next chapter, the NSLP districts lost between 11 and 28 percent of intended math and ELA instructional minutes because of classes starting late, ending early, or having prolonged disruptions. Pre-program training for both enrichment and academic teachers should include an explanation of the most common culprits for lost time, which we identify in Chapter Four, and model ways to teach "bell to bell."

Emphasize to Teachers That Engaging Academic Work Is a Part of Summer Fun

Because these programs are limited in duration, it is even more important that teachers have a sense of urgency in their attitude toward instruction. However, especially in the first two summers, we noted that districts' recruitment materials and teacher training promoted the summer programs as being like camp, emphasizing the enrichment and downplaying the academics. Although understandable, the implicit message was that academics were not an important part of the program and, if anything, dampened the fun. And each summer, we noted that some teachers adopted a "take it easy" attitude in the classroom because it was summer.

But taking a break from instruction did not necessarily result in a fun time for students. Rather, RAND observed that students appeared to have the best days when teachers used time in the classroom for engaging academic work. For more-detailed recommendations about time use, see Chapter Four. When training summer teachers, school district staff leading the training should

[T]aking a break from instruction did not necessarily result in a fun time for students. Rather, RAND observed that students appeared to have the best days when teachers used time in the classroom for engaging academic work.

highlight the academic and enrichment goals of the program and signal that protecting instructional time is a key way to achieve them.

Train Teachers to Effectively Check for Student Understanding

Checking for student understanding and adjusting instruction appropriately is an important way to promote learning. Teachers checked for understanding in fewer than half (46 percent) of the 263 mathematics and ELA classes we observed in summer 2014. For example, during independent practice, effective teachers checked each student's work; delivered brief one- to two-minute mini-lessons to struggling students; provided both positive and critical feedback; and kept circulating among all, not just some, students in the room to keep them on task.

Successful instances of teachers checking for student understanding relied on teachers having content knowledge to identify errors in the first place and then to offer alternative explanations to help clarify the concept. Teachers who appeared unfamiliar with the lesson for that day or unfamiliar with the content struggled to check successfully for understanding.

Teachers with poor classroom management skills often failed to successfully check all students for understanding, as well. Instead, these teachers tended to work with the one or two students who were the most off-task or the most confused during independent practice sessions and failed to check other students' work at all. Alternatively, teachers might check each students' work but only point out the fact that there was an error rather than working with that student to address the source of the misunderstanding.

Engage All Instructional Support Staff in Academic Training Sessions

All adults who will work in the academic classrooms need to understand the curriculum. Some districts provided a second adult in the academic classroom—usually a paraprofessional or, in some cases, a college student. When these instructors attended the curriculum training alongside the primary teacher, they could better support instruction by working in small groups or one on one with either struggling or advanced students. In the districts in which they were not included in the training, the additional person was more likely to engage almost exclusively in noninstructional tasks, such as distributing classroom materials, escorting students to the office, or administering a make-up assessment.

CHAPTER FOUR

Sufficient Time on Task

Students in the NSLP study who received at least 25 hours of math and 34 hours of language arts instruction in summer performed better on subsequent state exams. Unfortunately, intended time for instruction is easily lost. Summer program schedules and staff training can be designed to maximize the time dedicated to instruction.

Offering a program does not guarantee results. Productive academic learning time is more predictive of student achievement than the amount of student time in the classroom (Harnischfeger and Wiley, 1976; Lomax and Cooley, 1979; Fisher et al., 1980; Karweit and Slavin, 1982; Hawley et al., 1984; and Karweit, 1985). Therefore, how programs use time is critical. Summer programs that offer the same number of days can provide very different levels of average time on task depending on students' average daily attendance, the number of minutes assigned to class activities each day, the use of those intended instructional minutes, and the amount of time it takes to transition from one activity to the next. These elements combine to influence how many minutes of active class instruction children experience.

Figure 4.1 shows the substantial proportion of scheduled instructional hours for mathematics and ELA that were lost in summer 2014. It shows that a typical enrollee received anywhere from

FIGURE 4.1

Summer Attendees Received Substantially Less Instructional Time Than Intended

The combination of student absences and classes running shorter than scheduled took a big bite out of summer instructional hours.

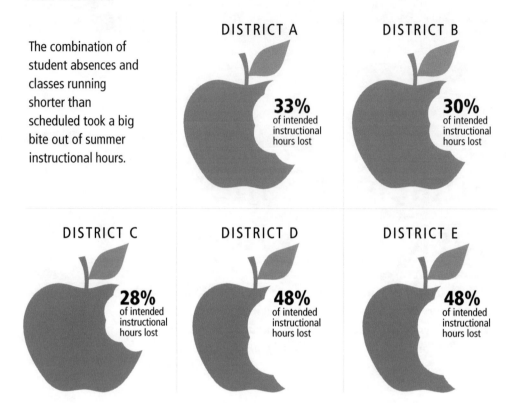

DISTRICT A

33% of intended instructional hours lost

DISTRICT B

30% of intended instructional hours lost

DISTRICT C

28% of intended instructional hours lost

DISTRICT D

48% of intended instructional hours lost

DISTRICT E

48% of intended instructional hours lost

SOURCES: Site schedules, student attendance, and RAND observation of time logs from summer 2014.

one-quarter to almost one-half fewer instructional minutes than intended, depending on the school district. Instructional minutes were lost to a combination of factors: classes that were shorter than scheduled, lost instructional time within the class, and students being absent at higher rates during the summer than during the school year. This held true in each of the four summers we observed, but we provide summer 2014 data to illustrate.

To understand how time is lost, consider District A, which lost one-third of intended instructional minutes (as shown in Figure 4.1). After factoring in such activities as field trips and plays, District A's printed summer program schedule had allotted 69 hours of academic instruction in summer 2014 (26 hours of math plus 43 hours of ELA). Based on the time logs collected during the more than 30 observation days RAND spent in District A, eight of those intended 69 hours (12 percent) were lost because of classes starting late; ending early; or having prolonged disruptions, such as off-topic conversations or bathroom breaks. This means a student in District A who had 100-percent attendance would have received approximately 61 combined hours of math and ELA instruction. But students in District A typically attended 78 percent of the program days, which reduced the 61 hours by another 13 because of student absence, leaving the typical attendee in District A with about 47 hours of combined math and ELA instruction. The 47 hours is 32 percent less than the intended 69 hours for math and ELA instruction.

Arguably, student absences are largely outside a program's control. Use of class minutes, however, is within its control. Looking across the five districts, we found as few as 11 percent and as many as 28 percent of scheduled minutes per district for mathematics and ELA were lost to classes starting late or ending early or to midstream interruptions. We observed as few as 0 and as many as 77 percent of scheduled minutes lost to noninstruction in a single mathematics or ELA class for these reasons. Box 4.1 uses examples drawn from observations at two pseudonymously named summer

BOX 4.1

The Influence of Master Schedules and Messaging on Protecting Instructional Time

The following two illustrations show how program and site leader decisions about scheduling and logistics plus communication about attendance can influence the amount of intended time devoted to instruction.

Staff at Pine Summer Site, including the bus driver, followed a common message: "on task and on time." In the spring, the site leader created a master schedule by first identifying the intended number of class minutes for mathematics, ELA, and enrichment each week, and then building a schedule that provided adequate time for breaks and transitions (which needed to be especially long at the outdoor campus). Having adequate transition times protected class time by allowing students and staff to arrive at each activity location on time. Classes not only started and ended on time but teachers also used an average of 97 percent of active class minutes for instruction. Students, in turn, demonstrated that they understood the expectations by remaining on task throughout the day.

By contrast, at Dogwood Summer Site, staff had a "take it easy" approach throughout the summer and used 76 percent of planned instructional time for instruction. The site's daily morning meeting ran late on one of the observation days, causing the first classes to start behind schedule. In addition, the schedule did not adequately account for transition time or bathroom breaks, causing classes to start as much as 15 minutes late. Teachers also allowed large amounts of down time for students to relax by socializing, further reducing intended instructional minutes.

sites to show how school district and site leader decisions can influence the amount of intended time devoted to instruction.

We make the following recommendations regarding time use to help ensure that students who attend receive at least the minimum instructional hours we found to be beneficial to student performance.

Operate the Program for Five to Six Weeks with Three to Four Hours of Academics per Day

SCHEDULING TIPS

Design your program to offer the number of instructional hours at which students benefited in the NSLP study.

Operate the program for at least five weeks.

Offer 90 minutes or more of math per day.

Offer 120 minutes or more of ELA per day.

Although the number of programming days depends on several factors, such as budget and time needed for school-year preparations (e.g., time to wrap up the prior school year, time to prepare for the next school year, and time to ensure school facilities receive summer maintenance), even a "long" summer program is just a fraction of a school year.

We recommend offering a program for at least five weeks. This length is to allow a typical student who attends 75 percent of program days to obtain the 25 hours of math and 34 hours of ELA instruction that we found in the NSLP study to be correlated with measurably improved achievement on subsequent state exams (Augustine et al., 2016). (We further assume there are 23 summer program days in a five-week period because of a holiday or a field trip and that a program offers 90 minutes of math per day and 120 minutes of ELA per day.)

Expert opinion on the optimal length of a summer program varies (McCombs et al., 2011); however, it appears that a minimum of five weeks might be a good and realistic guideline for districts to follow to maximize academic time on task. This number of weeks allows a few weeks of gap after the school year ends and before the next year begins while still giving students sufficient time on task in the summer programs.

Most NSLP summer programs offered 60–90 minutes of mathematics, 90–120 minutes of ELA, and 2–3 hours for enrichment activities per summer program day. We recommend the upper allocation of 90 minutes of mathematics and two hours of ELA daily because it would result in the amount of instruction at which we saw benefits for the typical attendee who came three out of every four summer program days and not just for the most-frequent attendees. The upper allocation would allow a student who attends 75 percent of the program (i.e., 19 out of 23 summer program days) to obtain more than 25 hours of mathematics and 34 hours of ELA instruction over the course of the summer program.

Provide Time for Transitions in the Master Schedule

When scheduling three to four hours a day for academics, it is important to acknowledge the time it takes for transitions from one class to the next. Adequately accounting for the needed minutes for students to transition from one activity to the next helps ensure that classes start and end on time. Schedules that failed to realistically account for transitions could have a ripple effect, such that classes grew progressively more delayed over the course of a day. Some teachers were forced to abandon the printed schedule and had to pick and choose what they could realistically cover from the curriculum. Master schedules that build in transition and break time help instructors and site leaders succeed at protecting class time. This could mean lengthening the summer program day to ensure the three to four hours for academic instruction.

Schedule Academic Classes to Occur in One Continuous Block

Scheduling academic classes in one continuous block minimizes the loss of instructional time that often accompanies class launch and wrap-up. In contrast, multipart classes that included scheduled breaks typically resulted in more lost time. For example, a mathematics class might begin before lunch, pause for lunch, and then resume after students finish eating. Of the classes we observed, multipart mathematics and ELA classes lost 27 class minutes on average (not including the pause), and single, continuous classes lost 15 minutes on average.[1] The majority of this "extra" time lost in multipart classes was a result of time spent transitioning to and from the classroom and within the classroom. These multipart classes lost additional minutes because they had multiple lesson launches and lesson winddowns during which minutes were spent handing out or collecting materials as students trickled in or out of the classroom.

> Almost two-thirds of classes that RAND observed in summer 2014 started late, one-third ended early, and one-fifth both started late and ended early. Furthermore, of the classes that started late, one-quarter started more than ten minutes late.

Minimize the Loss of Instructional Time by Attending to Summer Site Logistics

TOOL

See a sample master schedule at The Wallace Foundation's Summer Learning Toolkit (undated).

To launch instruction in the first class of the first day of the program, logistics need to run smoothly, which means, for example, that buses need to arrive on time and teachers need to have curriculum materials in hand. Late buses, meal delivery, and delivery of materials were widespread at summer sites in summer 2011 but lessened over time. At a minority of summer sites, there were ongoing logistical challenges resulting in lost instructional time. For example, because of missing supplies, some teachers had to share manuals, and some students had to share reading books in ELA or textbooks in mathematics, all of which slowed the pace of the lesson.

Communicate the Importance of Maximizing Instructional Time to Site Leaders

Site leaders influence the amount of academic time on task that students receive because they set the vision for, and climate of, the site's program. In some districts, site leaders also set arrival and departure times, created the daily schedule, and ensured availability of supplies. Regardless of whether the central office summer program leaders or site leaders create the master schedules for the summer sites, the program leaders should communicate to site leads not only a timetable and process for logistics but also the vision and goals for the program, including the importance of sufficient time on task to achieve positive outcomes for students.

Of the classes we observed, multipart mathematics and ELA classes lost 27 class minutes on average (not including the pause), and single, continuous classes lost 15 minutes on average.

Provide Teachers with Strategies for Maximizing Instructional Time

Classes in which teachers efficiently used time not only covered more content but also better sustained student interest. For example, an average of 86 percent of ELA time was spent on instruction during days that RAND observers rated both student enjoyment and instructional quality as high. In contrast, an average of only 60 percent of ELA class minutes was spent on instruction during days that RAND observers rated both student enjoyment and instructional quality as low.

Although well-structured bell schedules were a big help to classes

---

[1] We observed 109 mathematics or ELA classes that were multipart and 154 continuous mathematics or ELA classes in summer 2014.

starting and ending on time, teachers' choices also influenced the amount of productive academic time students experienced during the minutes when class was in session. Based on our detailed classroom observation time logs from summer 2014, we noticed three common points at which teachers frequently lost instructional minutes, as follows:

- **Opening and closing of class.** Minutes were lost during the launch and wrap-up of class. Launching and wrapping up will necessarily take at least some noninstructional time as students get out or put away materials or teachers write instructions on a board or take attendance. But the class launches and closings we observed ranged substantially in their efficiency. Teachers who used time well typically established predictable, clear classroom routines, such as proceeding quickly from desks to the class rug or filing into class and immediately hanging up bags on hooks. In well-managed classes, students clearly knew the routine and behavior expectations. For example, class helpers quickly passed out materials, and students went to assigned seats or immediately started with the expected warm-up activity.

- **Afternoon slump.** Minutes were also lost during the "afternoon slump," when the pace of the post-lunch classes was often slower than during the morning classes. On average in summer 2014, observed ELA and mathematics classes occurring after 12 p.m. lost 20–23 percent of scheduled instructional time; those occurring before noon lost an average of 13–15 percent. However, this pattern was not true across the board. Some teachers made good use of afternoon time: nearly one-half of mathematics classes and roughly one-quarter of observed ELA classes ran efficiently in the afternoon, with less than 5 percent of intended minutes lost.

- **Independent practice.** The third and most significant way that active class minutes were lost was during independent practice time, which is the single class activity in which students most easily got distracted and off track. Almost every academic class we observed included independent practice: 94 percent of mathematics and 91 percent of ELA classes. These classes devoted substantial time to independent practice: an average of 36 minutes of class time in mathematics and 45 minutes in ELA per day. Teachers' efficient use of

> We noticed three common points at which teachers frequently lost instructional minutes.

> **TRAINING TIP**
>
> Summer professional development sessions and coaches can demonstrate and offer examples of efficient start-up and wind-down classroom routines.

independent practice distinguished the best-rated from the lowest-rated classes (see Box 4.2). For example, most students were on task for an average of 95 percent of independent practice minutes in the ELA classes that RAND observers rated in summer 2014 as outstanding, compared with only 55 percent of independent practice minutes in the ELA classes that RAND observers rated as poor. The same trend held for mathematics classes.

BOX 4.2

Five tips for an on-track independent practice session

Examining our minute-by-minute logs of prolonged time loss (seven minutes or longer) during ELA independent practice sessions helped us develop the following tips:

1. Circulate among all, not some, students throughout the entire independent practice.

2. Offer planned activities for students who finished the primary assignment early.

3. Offer activities that are neither too challenging nor monotonous, which are two circumstances in which students routinely struggled to stay focused.

4. Avoid using independent practice time for miscellaneous housekeeping, such as collecting permission slips, starting an off-topic conversion, or initiating an unscheduled break.

5. During independent silent reading, work with struggling readers in a small-group format. Although strong readers read voraciously during independent silent reading times, struggling readers often appeared to not be reading at all.

CHAPTER FIVE

Student Recruitment and Attendance

Students cannot benefit if they do not sign up and attend regularly. The combination of recruitment materials, attendance policies, and attendance incentives can help ensure that students benefit from summer programs.

O ffering a program with high-quality instruction is insufficient to improve student achievement: Districts also need to attract students to the program and students then need to show up and attend consistently. Our research concluded that if students attended the program that we studied for at least 20 days over the course of the summer, they experienced academic benefits (Augustine et al., 2017). Consequently, developing effective recruitment materials and accurate attendance-taking systems are important to ensure that students benefit. In this chapter, we offer recommendations on student recruitment and attendance based on best practices from the NSLP districts.

Acknowledge That Consistent Attendance Is Possible in Different Types of Summer Programs

In the summer learning field, program designers debate whether camp-like programs that "mask" learning have stronger attendance than more-traditional programs that have explicit academic objectives. In our study, we did not see a relationship between the type of program and attendance. Across the four summers, the two districts with the highest average daily attendance rates featured a program structured like the school year and a program designed like a camp. The traditional program devoted the most hours to academics and the least hours to enrichment; the camp-like program focused heavily on enrichment experiences and worked to strengthen students' social and emotional well-being in addition to improving academic achievement. Because we saw high attendance in both types of summer programs, we do not recommend one over the other for recruitment or attendance purposes, although we do recommend three to four hours a day of academics, as described in Chapter Four.

Develop Accurate and Timely Recruitment Materials

The most effective recruitment process we observed paired materials that accurately explained requirements and program features up front with some personalized recruitment.

Regardless of the style of summer program, we suspect that not accurately describing the program to families could lower attendance and future summer participation. In its summer 2013 enrollment materials, one of the districts focused only on the "fun" enrichment activities and did not highlight the academic component of the program. Interviewees in this district reported that some students were surprised and disappointed by the content of the program relative to what was advertised. In this same district, 13 percent of students who attended at least one day in the first week dropped out of the program, compared with a drop-out rate of 2–7-percent for the first week in the other four districts. Re-registration rates for the second summer were also far lower in this district (52 percent) than in others (70–82 percent).

In addition to accuracy, the timeliness of information is also important, particularly in reducing no-show rates. During the months leading up to summer 2013, districts and their partners initiated more-concerted efforts than they had done in the prior summer to send families information about program acceptance, transportation routes, and the program schedule. Some districts sent a robocall from the superintendent to families as a reminder the day before the program was to start. There was a lower no-show rate in summer 2013 than there had been in summer 2012, which we suspect was driven by these efforts.

Personalize Recruitment of Students and Their Families

The most effective recruitment process we observed paired materials that accurately explained requirements and program features up front with some personalized recruitment. The districts with the lowest no-show rates in 2013 made personal connections with families in their program reminders. In one district, summer teachers sent a handwritten letter to the student's class to welcome the student to the program and classroom. In another district, a coordinator at the students' school talked with families and students, reminding them of the upcoming program and explaining its benefits.

Establish a Firm Enrollment Deadline

To determine how many staff to hire and to create classes, districts need to know how many students have enrolled. Although there is an understandable desire to serve all students who need the program regardless of when they sign up, there are high costs to a rolling enrollment policy and distinct benefits to setting enrollment deadlines. We have already pointed out that enrollment deadlines are necessary for program planning: When districts can predict enrollment, they can also assign students to classrooms, assign teachers to students, and plan bus routes.

But setting enrollment cutoff dates is important for other reasons as well: It ensures higher average daily attendance rates and improves learning. Districts without enrollment deadlines (e.g., those allowing students to enroll in week two of the program) implicitly send a message to students and parents that regular attendance in the program is not necessary. If a student enrolls halfway through the program, it would be impossible for that student to have an average daily attendance rate of more than 50 percent, with implications for learning. Moreover, some interviewees suggested that open enrollment conveyed the wrong message to parents. As one interviewee in 2011 explained, "The district feels that anyone can enroll at any time, so it's hard to say, 'You can't miss any days.'"

> There is an understandable desire to serve all students who need the program regardless of when they sign up, there are high costs to a rolling enrollment policy and distinct benefits to setting enrollment deadlines.

Over the course of the NSLP, the programs instituted firm enrollment deadlines and realized several advantages in addition to stronger average daily attendance:

- Parents can be notified in advance of transportation routes. Not having children's home addresses ahead of time forced sites into establishing routes and notifying parents and even bus drivers of bus stop locations sometimes within 24 hours of the program's start.

- Districts can staff the program to meet desired student-to-adult ratios and better vet staff instead of making last-minute hires or staff releases when actual and projected enrollments differ. In summer 2011, one district was off by 43 percent on enrollment projections, leading teachers to postpone launching their curricula until program leaders shuffled teachers and students to balance classes by size.

- Teachers learn who their students are before the program starts.

- Students can be equally distributed across classrooms and grouped according to performance, if desired.

Establish a Clear Attendance Policy

Setting clear expectations is an important step to achieving good attendance because parents might otherwise assume that attendance at summer programs is optional. Districts that stated in their application and orientation materials that daily attendance was expected typically had more success in this regard. For instance, in one district, students who missed more than three days of the summer program could be asked to leave the program. Site leaders called parents when students were absent. This district had a high average daily attendance rate across all four summers (more than 81 percent on average).

Track the Number of Initial Enrollees Who Never Attend, as Well as Summer Attendees' Daily Attendance

Accurate summer attendance data help districts both know how many hires to make and track the amount of instruction that students receive. Districts and sites should track two aspects of student attendance: the no-show rate of students who sign up for the summer program but never attend and the daily attendance of enrollees who do participate. Reducing no-show rates and increasing attendance rates gives more students the instructional time that we found was associated with subsequent improved performance. In addition, tracking no-show rates from year to year facilitates planning and teacher hiring. Hiring adults based on projected attendance rates is more cost-efficient than hiring based on the number of students who initially sign up for the program.

Our data suggest that districts had more success lowering no-show rates over time than boosting average daily attendance at summer programs. The student recruitment strategies we have described—such as reminders about program acceptance, robo-calls, timely communication, and even hand-written notes from teachers to admitted students—helped reduce no-shows to as low as 8 percent of enrollees in summer 2013, compared with 32 percent in another district that did not adopt a personalized way to remind families of the program and its logistical details. But our data suggest that several factors contributing to inconsistent summer attendance are harder for schools to fully address: an attitude that summer programs should be and are more relaxed than the school year, thus allowing for dropping in and out of the summer session; a need for students to care for younger siblings at home; changes to family vacation plans; student dislike of the program; and competing alternatives.

To improve attendance, we suggest student incentives (described in the next recommendation), as well as attendance policies and clear communication in advance of the program that daily attendance is expected among all who sign up. Tracking daily attendance allows summer program leaders to enforce their attendance requirements and to place calls home to parents to encourage their children to attend.

If Resources Allow, Provide Incentives to Parents and Students for Attendance

Many districts offer some type of incentive to encourage strong attendance in voluntary summer programs. Based on an experiment we conducted in 2012 in one of the five NSLP summer programs, we recommend that, if resources allow, districts offer a combination of parent and student incentives for attendance (see

TOOL

For a sample student attendance tracker, visit The Wallace Foundation's Summer Learning Toolkit (undated).

Box 5.1). This combination increased attendance by 5 percentage points compared with a group of students in the same program whose families were not offered incentives (Martorell et al., 2016). Parents were offered a $50 gift card to a local supermarket based on student attendance during the first two weeks of the program, and another $70 card based on student attendance during the last two and a half weeks. Students, meanwhile, got to earn small prizes at the end of each week based on attending four or five days in that week. The combination of parent and student incentives had a larger impact on attendance than when only students (and not parents) were offered incentives.

We note, however, that the incentives were costly; the district spent $15,000 on the student incentives (distributed to those out of approximately 2,500 students who had sufficiently high attendance) and an additional $54,000 on parent incentives. Incentives as generous as these are not always budgetarily feasible for districts. Combined, they cost $67 for each additional day of student attendance (Martorell et al., 2016).

Summer program leaders in the NSLP have advocated lower-cost alternatives, such as field trips and other student rewards for participation, which they think improved attendance rates. For example, several districts required that students attend a certain number of days during the week of a field trip to participate in it. Some districts also used small incentives, such as public recognition, treats, games, and parties as rewards for strong attendance. Also, a district that previously offered a voluntary program that offered only academics thought that the addition of enrichment classes and a full day of programming had increased attendance rates substantially. Student incentives might be more powerful when combined with attendance expectations and an enrollment cutoff, a finding corroborated by other programs' experiences (McCombs et al., 2011).

We note, however, that enforcing attendance at voluntary summer programs remained a challenge for NSLP districts even with explicit attendance policies and the use of combined strategies (such as incentives and daily phone calls home). Regardless of districts' attendance policies, students' average daily attendance in the summer was lower than their school-year attendance rates in each of the four summers in each of the five NSLP districts. During each of the four summers in the NSLP, students who attended at least one day typically attended about 75 percent of the time, and about 60 percent of students attended 20 or more days of their program. However, there was variation in attendance rates among the districts, where, for example, average daily attendance ranged from 69 to 84 percent in summer 2013. It was not until a summer program mandated attendance for grade advancement (which one district did in summer 2011 and 2012) that summer program attendance rates reached school-year rates. Although the combination of attendance incentives and policies boost summer attendance somewhat, it is unlikely they will affect attendance rates during the summer so that they are comparable with school-year rates.

BOX 5.1

Attendance Tip: Combine Strategies to Maximize Attendance

One district with a six-week summer program set a clear attendance policy in all its promotional materials: Students were not to miss more than three days because they needed to attend to benefit from the program. In addition, the policy established incentives for students to encourage attendance, including an attendance threshold to participate in field trips. Each site also designed its own student incentive scheme that included weekly events for classrooms with high attendance, such as ice cream treats, pizza parties, dance parties, and candy rewards. One site held a water day with water slides and a dunking booth for regular attendees. According to site leaders, teachers, and enrichment staff, these incentives worked. Site leaders reported that, with these incentives in place, what had been historically large dips in attendance after the Fourth of July were smaller.

Academic Curricula and Instruction

Summer programs are short and often provide little time for teachers to plan their lessons. To maximize the effectiveness of instruction, teachers should have both high-quality curriculum materials that are matched to student needs and small class sizes.

There are several reasons why selecting curricula for the summer is challenging, including that there are few summer-specific commercial curricula to choose from. Many districts, therefore, adapt school-year curricula for the summer, which entails significant work to ensure that the learning goals align to the summer time frame and that units are selected appropriately. In this chapter, we provide recommendations on summer program curricula and their implementation.

Whether districts opt to purchase commercially developed curricula, develop them in-house, or extend the school-year curricula into the summer, having a single curriculum for each subject that all summer program sites follow benefits students and maximizes resources. A common curriculum helps prevent inconsistency (and inequity) in student experiences. In most of the districts we studied, there was one centrally purchased or developed

> Whether districts opt to purchase commercially developed curricula, develop them in-house, or extend the school-year curricula into the summer, having a single curriculum for each subject that all summer program sites follow benefits students and maximizes resources.

curriculum per subject that all teachers across the district followed in the summer. These districts had the strongest curricula. Teachers found lesson plans clear and easy to follow, and all students throughout the program were typically exposed to the same amount of instruction, targeted toward the same knowledge and skill development.

The example in Box 6.1 shows how written curricula can reduce the burden on teachers, standardize content across classrooms, and improve staff perceptions of summer program organization.

BOX 6.1

Providing a Written Curriculum for Each Subject Increases the Content Covered, Supports Better Use of Instructional Time, and Reduces Burden on Teachers

In its first summer, District A opted for teachers to self-develop their own lessons. This choice reflected the district's ethos of decentralized decisionmaking and empowerment of teachers, but summer teachers described insufficient time to develop lessons, increased workload, and dissatisfaction with resulting lessons.

Although the quality of teachers selected for the program was generally high, teachers in District A in summer 2011 covered the least amount of content and had the most amount of time lost during class of the five school districts. Of the 17 teacher interviews that we conducted in District A that summer, only three felt positive about how their lessons went that day. The other 14 were ambivalent or thought that the lessons went poorly, typically because of lack of time for planning. Most teachers we interviewed had few academic learning objectives for the summer, and many did not write lesson plans. Furthermore, many teachers cited lack of curriculum as a major reason to not return to teach in the next summer.

Upon adopting standardized curricula in summer 2012, District A substantially improved academic instruction. We observed much better organized and clearer lessons in summer 2012 than in summer 2011. And in 2012, District A had the least amount of time lost to noninstructional activities during academic blocks of the five school districts in the study. Teacher and site leader satisfaction also increased. As one site leader noted in an interview:

> *I think one big advantage this year was having a curriculum provided. That was a big plus, because trying to create curriculum out of air is very difficult, if not impossible.*

Engage Experts to Anchor the Program in Written Curricula That Align with School-Year Standards and Students' Needs

If Purchasing Curricula, Adapt Them to Fit Student Needs and Available Instructional Time

A district curriculum expert could decide to purchase commercially developed curricula for the summer program because those curricula have the benefit of offering coherent courses of study designed for four to six weeks of instruction. For example, the American Reading Company–Summer Semester curriculum used in two of the NSLP districts included language arts lesson plans and the materials needed to implement them, such as grade-level books on the theme of each unit for teachers to use for the informational read-aloud component of the lesson and 20 nonfiction books related to the unit or theme organized in baskets according to reading levels. Students used information from these books to write their own books, which was the culminating product of the summer session (e.g., a book on frogs at a summer site where the American Reading Company theme was animals).

We recommend that districts adapt purchased curricula before distributing them to teachers so that the lesson plans fit the amount of instructional time available in the summer program, align to district school-year standards, and fit the district's student needs. Although commercially produced curricula should be targeted to the duration of a typical summer program, they might not perfectly align with the hours available in any given summer program. Teachers frequently reported in interviews and surveys that the summer curricula included more content than it was possible to cover. RAND observers also noted occasions when there was insufficient material to fill the entire class period. This meant that summer teachers had to decide on their own what content to skip, alter, or add. Adaptation by school district curriculum designers ahead of the summer session could help to ensure that the intended material is taught. A short survey of summer teachers about the strengths and shortcomings of the curriculum could help district curriculum designers adapt and improve the curriculum each summer.

We recommend that districts adapt purchased curricula before distributing them to teachers so that the lesson plans fit the amount of instructional time available in the summer program, align to district school-year standards, and fit the district's student needs.

If Developing Curricula, Work with District Curriculum Design Experts and Start Early

Other districts opt to develop summer curricula in-house. Program leaders who do so should involve district curriculum writers months before the summer program starts, particularly if the program targets a wide variety of students. Curriculum development is time-intensive and best done by curriculum experts. District experts can develop summer curricula that is coherent, comprehensive, and aligns with or extends the school-year curriculum.

> When the curriculum department was involved in writing the curriculum, it was more clearly aligned to school-year systems, goals, and content . . . And, by basing curricula on existing materials, districts were able to reduce the costs of buying materials . . . as well as avoid mishaps with late delivery or lost resources. (Augustine and Thompson, 2017, p. 35)

Districts that told teachers to develop their own lessons or that provided stipends to teachers for developing summer curricula encountered several pitfalls. In the districts that developed their own summer curricula by providing teachers with stipends, those teachers struggled to write them on time. In one such district, lesson plans were photocopied for teachers just minutes before classes were to begin, meaning that they were not available during the scheduled teacher training on the curriculum. In another district using this approach, the resulting curriculum was not coherent and included materials that were not aligned with students' abilities. In a district that had individual teachers developing their own lessons, not all students experienced the same amount of instructional time or type of instruction across sites. We also observed that some academic teachers prioritized their own topics (e.g., leadership development skills) over mathematics or ELA instruction. Given the constraints on teachers' time, it is not surprising that two external reviewers of summer 2011 curricula judged the commercial summer curricula to be of higher quality than those developed either by the summer teachers or a teacher on assignment.

Provide Strategies for Differentiation in Curriculum Materials

The summer curriculum should provide materials for subgroups of students, including those who need more practice with the content and those who need more-advanced material to extend the content. Even in summer programs targeting low-performing students, surveyed teachers reported large differences in knowledge and skills among students and struggles to ensure that their lessons appropriately challenged everyone in their classrooms. Having differentiated materials (e.g., lesson plans and activities for specific students based on aptitude) is particularly important during independent practice time, which was provided in the large majority of ELA and mathematics classes we observed. Differentiated instruction during independent practice time allowed students who quickly completed tasks to extend their learning while also allowing students who struggled to gain additional support. A minority of summer curricula provided materials for teachers to use to differentiate their lessons during the summer program. We observed very few teachers supplementing the curriculum materials with activities of their own making.

Encourage Instructional Leaders to Observe Instruction of the Curriculum and Provide Feedback

Providing instructional leadership supports teachers and aids student learning. Some summer site leaders routinely observed teachers' summer classes while others rarely or never did so. In keeping with the message that strong academics contribute to summer fun, program leaders should encourage their site leaders to provide instructional leadership by observing teachers' classes, providing them with feedback, and building in time for teachers to confer with one another about practices. These methods should be effective if the site leader has past instructional leadership experiences. We also recommend encouraging curriculum designers and coaches to observe instruction so they can see how the curriculum works in practice and develop adaptations for the current and future summers. Some summer programs assigned academic coaches to each site to observe instruction and provide feedback. In other programs, coaches were hired centrally and visited the sites on a rotating basis, also observing teachers, providing feedback, and offering some on-site professional development throughout the summer.

> Districts that told teachers to develop their own lessons or that provided stipends to teachers for developing summer curricula encountered several pitfalls.

Serve Students in Small Classes or Groups

With a small class, a teacher can more quickly establish rapport with students, get to know their individual learning needs, and provide more individualized attention. In the classrooms we observed, there were no more than 15 students per adult instructor. Interviewed teachers appreciated these small class sizes, noting that summer was a time when they could reach students who could "hide" during the school year. These were students who were not performing well but not misbehaving and therefore did not attract attention from their teachers during the year. With relatively long independent practice periods of 30 minutes or more, such as we routinely observed in NSLP summer classes, teachers had time to work with these students in the summer program.

CHAPTER SEVEN

Enrichment Activities and Their Implementation

If programs are to provide engaging enrichment experiences for students, they must be as well planned and as high quality as the academics.

Research confirms that lower-income children are less likely than their higher-income peers to engage in enrichment activities—such as art or music lessons; vacations; and visits to museums, zoos, libraries, or other educational venues (Alexander, Entwisle, and Olson, 2001; Chin and Phillips, 2004; Wimer et al., 2006). These disparities can come into particularly sharp focus during the summer months, when there are few free activities for children and youth.

To address this gap, each of the districts offered full-day programming that included enrichment classes. In some districts, these were novel activities not typically offered in school, such as kayaking, ropes courses, swimming, or karate. In other districts, enrichment activities included subjects offered during school, such as art and music.

The NSLP districts had three main reasons for prominently featuring enrichment in their summer programs. First, as noted earlier, districts desired to increase access to and participation in enrichment activities to reduce the opportunity gap facing many children from low-income families during the summer. Second, these activities were considered essential for attracting student enrollees and encouraging consistent attendance. Third, teachers generally felt that providing enrichment helped a child's personal development, and many mentioned that it was a needed corrective to a school year that crowds out time for these activities. Some emphasized that enrichment activities developed the child's self-confidence, an outcome that should improve academic performance as well. For example, one teacher told us, "I am seeing kids grow in ways that on paper are not academic growth. I am seeing them grow as stewards of nature and as investigators."

In our observations, we found that high-quality enrichment opportunities contributed to fun and enjoyable days for students. To determine the quality of enrichment classes, RAND observers considered efficient use of time, clear instruction, teacher engagement, student participation, and student enjoyment. Box 7.1 shows the difference for students between a well-managed enrichment experience and a poorly managed one.

In this chapter, we recommend steps that districts and their partners can take to help ensure that enrichment is well managed and of high quality.

Select a Model for Providing Enrichment Activities

Each district followed one of three models in providing enrichment activities, and we found that all of these approaches worked when implemented well by qualified staff. In some cases, the different approaches reflected the different objectives of the districts and resulted in different types of activities. Those districts that pursued outside partnerships did it to expand the program offerings to students to help reduce the "opportunity gap" between students from low- and higher-income families during the summer and to reduce the overall costs of the summer program. Factors including cost and capacity of CBO partners also influenced the selected delivery model. In each type of arrangement, we observed high-quality enrichment when the instructor was actively engaged throughout, had content knowledge, enforced student behavior rules that were consistent with the academic portion of the

> Each district followed one of three models in providing enrichment activities, and we found that all of these approaches worked when implemented well by qualified staff.

BOX 7.1

Enrichment Teachers with Strong Content Knowledge Provide High-Quality, Engaging Experiences for Youth: Dance Class Experiences

In the strong dance class, the teacher had prior experience and knowledge of dance, demonstrated the activities herself, closely monitored students as they practiced, tried to keep all students involved, held students accountable for taking it seriously, encouraged students as they learned, and connected the lesson to content that students were learning in other classes. As a result, students worked to learn the dance and had fun while doing so. In the poor dance class, by contrast, the teacher did not have prior experience with dance, lacked strong classroom management skills, and was disconnected from students. She offered no direct instruction, made no attempt to engage students, held no one accountable for participating, and occasionally checked her phone. As a result, many students did not participate in the dance and most appeared bored.

Strong dance class

Ms. G launched the lesson by asking students whether they had any ideas about dances that come from the continent that students were learning about in academic classes. Ms. G then stated the day's activity, which was a miniature audition for the culminating production. She named the dance steps they would learn (rhumba steps from Cuba) and explained and modeled how the most important part of the dance is to switch your weight from side to side. Students lined up and practiced the steps, first with the teacher demonstrating and then with students trying them alone. When the boys and girls made faces about dancing together, Ms. G reminded students that making faces and giggling were not acceptable behaviors. All students danced while Ms. G actively monitored the children, requesting that one boy take a break because he was not taking it seriously and inviting him back to the group after one minute. At the end of class, Ms. G praised students' efforts: "I really appreciate your hard work today. I know it has been a long practice."

Poor dance class

After launching the lesson by telling the fifth-grade students they would do some dance exercises, Ms. L put on two videos while students crowded together to watch. Ms. L stood in the front watching the screen instead of the students, appearing as though she was teaching herself the steps while watching the videos. As she moved, she held her phone and looked at it periodically. A teacher's aide stood at the front but looked at her phone throughout, and it was not clear whether the aide was supposed to be part of the class. Ms. L offered no instruction and did not direct the students to practice during the videos. Some students followed along with the videos, but, overall, students appeared bored. During the second video, Ms. L commented to one student, "I can tell you're having a good time" and the boy replied, "Psh, no." Once the second video ended, students took a water break and talked freely for the remaining seven minutes of class. During this time, Ms. L told the fifth-grade students that the second-graders did the dance better than they did.

program, and led students through sequenced activities, as we discuss in the following recommendations:

- **Approach 1: Hire district teachers.** Two districts hired teachers who worked for the district during the school year to provide enrichment activities to students during the summer at several sites. Enrichment activities provided in these districts were often similar to what schools might offer during the school year—visual art, music, drama, and physical education—but also included classes not featured during the school year, such as yoga and dance.

- **Approach 2: Contract directly with enrichment providers.** One district issued a request for proposals in August, and initial proposals from CBOs were submitted in November. Responding CBOs were required to develop an enrichment curriculum that included the reinforcement of academic skills, a schedule, learning goals for the students, projections of the number of students who could be served, and a budget. In its attempt to narrow the opportunity gap, this district offered a wide variety of programming across multiple grades, which included fencing, swimming, studio art, biking, science, and drama.

- **Approach 3: Establish strategic partnerships with intermediaries.** Two districts partnered with intermediary organizations, which pair up individual providers and provider organizations with school districts and then manage these partnerships. These intermediaries selected CBOs and individual providers. In one district, the intermediary hired both district fine arts teachers and local artists to provide arts-based enrichment, and the program featured both an explicit block integrating arts and academics and a studio arts period. In the other district, the intermediary brokered partnerships between local CBOs and schools, and each CBO was responsible for its own summer program. These programs offered both off-site activities (such as tennis, sailing, and outdoor natural science activities) and activities that took place in the school building (such as swimming, computer education, and arts and crafts). Each of these CBOs hired its enrichment teachers and developed its own enrichment curricula.

[E]nrichment teachers with strong content knowledge more frequently demonstrated and modeled skills, corrected student techniques, and built on student strengths.

Ensure That Enrichment Instructors Have Strong Content Knowledge

Content knowledge is the backbone of an effective lesson. Regardless of the approach used to provide enrichment, instructors with strong content knowledge led classes that appeared more effective and engaging than teachers who lacked sufficient content knowledge (as illustrated in Box 7.1). Specifically, enrichment teachers with strong content knowledge more frequently demonstrated and modeled skills, corrected student techniques, and built on student strengths. For example, a music teacher grouped students by their natural pitch (e.g., altos and sopranos) and demonstrated various pitches, a dance teacher adjusted the choreography to accommodate students' various levels of ability and gradually added new movements, and a physical education coach modeled soccer techniques and provided guidance during student play. In contrast, enrichment teachers with minimal content knowledge introduced an activity but were unprepared to adjust the activity, demonstrate skills, or work to increase student engagement. Job descriptions should expressly require active co-participation and facilitation of the enrichment activities that instructors lead.

> During the four summers of the study, we observed higher rates of student misbehavior and off-task behavior during enrichment than we did during academic classes.

Train Enrichment Instructors in Behavior Management and Monitor Its Implementation

Student misbehavior detracts from time that can be better spent on instruction and practice. During the four summers of the study, we observed higher rates of student misbehavior and off-task behavior during enrichment than we did during academic classes. We noted that misbehavior often stemmed from lack of activity (e.g., waiting in line for many minutes to get a short turn), poor or no directions when launching the activity, and instructors who were not versed in classroom management techniques. The enrichment instructors—who ranged from high school and college students to experienced professionals—did not always have experience instructing groups of young students, and the high school student instructors sometimes visibly struggled with adopting a role of authority. In some districts, academic teachers and enrichment instructors did not share the same rules or enforce the same behavioral expectations, which was particularly evident when students transitioned from morning academics with teachers (who were present only in the morning) to afternoon enrichment with different instructors.

To improve behavior management during enrichment periods, we recommend professional development for enrichment instructors that models (and not just states) behavior management strategies. Behavior management rules for school and enrichment activities should be written down with similar or the same expectations and consequences during the school and enrichment portions of the day.

We also recommend that site leaders monitor enrichment staff to ensure that they have support to enact the program's behavior management policies. These observations can boost the quality of the enrichment by providing enrichment instructors with support in classroom management techniques and successful instruction, and they can ensure continuity of messages and instruction across the academic and enrichment portions of the summer program day. By summer 2014, we observed that site directors were more present during the transition from academics to enrichment, helping to smooth student discipline and enforce greater continuity in norms and rules.

Plan Lessons to Include Sequenced Activities

TOOL

For a sample enrichment lesson plan, visit The Wallace Foundation's Summer Learning Toolkit (undated).

Good enrichment classes include activities that are organized, engaging, and sequenced and allow for the majority of students to actively participate for the duration of the class period. Even in the enrichment classes that were more "school-like," such as visual arts, we observed quality classes featuring sequenced activities (i.e., connected step by step) that built on each other during and across classes and required active effort from students throughout the class. In addition, these classes provided a context for the activity or skill (e.g., teachers showed pictures of hand-woven baskets to introduce a specific weaving style, displayed examples of various painting techniques, or explained stretches and exercises as they modeled them). These findings comport with other research indicating that successful enrichment activities have features that are "SAFE"—sequenced, active, focused, and explicit (Durlak and DuPre, 2008).

In comparison, in low-quality enrichment classes, activities were often poorly organized, conveyed little content, required only low or short bursts of effort from students, or excluded the majority of students from actively participating. For example, we observed enrichment classes with interesting topics (e.g., "science of money") that presented students with mundane activities that were not sufficient to occupy students' attention for the duration of the class period, such as cutting shapes out of construction paper, coloring a nametag, or a game that allowed only a few students to participate while most students sat with nothing to do.

Plan Carefully If Enrichment Is Integrated with Academics

Not all enrichment activities need or should be linked to academic content. But districts pursuing this goal are more likely to succeed if they conduct careful planning, offer specific curriculum guidance and additional training, and promote greater coordination between academic and enrichment staff.

The best examples of the integration of academic content and enrichment we observed were those in which academic content was naturally embedded in the enrichment activity, such as drama class (where students were reading and writing), music class (where students used fractions to measure rhythms), and nature explorations (in which students applied science concepts).

There were numerous other examples in which the combination of academic content and enrichment was less successful. Sometimes this occurred because the academic content was not a natural fit with the enrichment activity. For instance, in one archery lesson, the goal was to have students multiply two-digit numbers by multiplying the number of times students shot an arrow that hit the target. However, students hit the target so few times that the class wound up multiplying single digits. In another case, we observed lessons in which students were asked to imitate weather patterns through dance. However, the lesson lacked both the science of the weather patterns and formal dance instruction. These efforts resulted in poor-quality academic and enrichment instruction. The other main reasons that integration failed, according to enrichment instructors, was because instructors lacked written lesson plans and were not provided enough guidance on how to integrate or reinforce academic content successfully and meaningfully into lessons. As a result, both academic and enrichment content suffered.

Keep Class Sizes Small

Enrichment classes benefit from smaller class sizes in the same way that academic classes do. As with academic classes, we recommend class sizes of no more than 15 students for the enrichment activities. Although each of the districts maintained small class sizes in academic classes throughout the four years of the study, two of the districts combined classes of students for enrichment in 2011, resulting in far larger class sizes. In these classes, we observed difficulties with disruptive students. Half to three-quarters of enrichment instructors from summer 2011 in each of the two districts where this occurred reported that student misbehavior resulted in wasted instructional time, compared with only about one-quarter of enrichment instructors in districts with smaller class sizes.

CHAPTER EIGHT

Positive Summer Climate

Positive site climate drives student daily experiences and enjoyment of the program and is correlated with higher student attendance.

A program's climate reflects the site norms, goals, values, relationships, teaching and learning practices, and organizational structures (National School Climate Center, undated). The decisions made during planning about teacher selection, program scheduling, student recruitment, curriculum, and enrichment offerings all come together to influence the quality and character of a summer program.

Summer sites with consistently positive climates offered students an inclusive, friendly place where staff remained engaged with students throughout the day. In addition to promoting positive youth experiences, a positive climate also appeared to promote regular attendance. For example, in one district, average daily attendance in summer 2014 was 86 percent at sites where RAND observers consistently rated students as appearing to enjoy themselves, compared with a 79-percent average daily attendance rate where RAND observers consistently rated students as not enjoying themselves.[1]

Clarity, consistency, warmth, and engagement were the hallmarks of sites where RAND observers noted that students enjoyed their

---

[1] The site observers did not know the attendance rates at the sites they were observing.

day. Academic and enrichment teachers were actively engaged with students throughout the day, including during transitions and mealtimes. Staff were generally consistent in the way they enforced student behavior rules. Program leadership sets the tone of a site by structuring a well-organized program with clear roles and responsibilities among staff.

The examples in Box 8.1 are drawn from daylong observations at two pseudonymously named summer sites to show the contrast between positive and negative climates; they demonstrate how both class time and "in-between" time influence student experiences throughout a summer program day.

To identify the policy and programmatic differences between sites that created enjoyable student experiences in summer 2014 and those that failed to do so, we consulted our notes from RAND observers' daily site surveys, classroom observations, and staff interviews. We also examined the correlations between RAND observers' daily ratings of student enjoyment of the day and the other items from the daily site survey from each of the several days we observed each site. These analyses led to the recommendations we provide.[2]

Train All Staff on the Importance of Positive Adult Engagement with Students Throughout the Day—Not Only in Classes

> At sites with the strongest site cultures, staff and students shared a common language about the goals and culture of the program.

Not surprisingly, engaged adults make summer programs more enjoyable for students. Of the six items that RAND observers rated at the end of each summer observation day, the quality of staff-to-student interactions was the item most strongly and consistently related to whether students appeared to enjoy the day. On each day that students appeared to have an outstanding day (i.e., a 5 rating on the five-point scale from the observer's daily site survey), RAND observers found that instructional and noninstructional staff members were kind to students during not only active class time but also transition times and meals. For example, we observed teachers who engaged with students during recess to play a game of tag or organized games during breaks—all of which helped to build rapport with students. As

---

[2] At the end of each observation day in summer 2014, the RAND observer rated the statement "Students appeared to have enjoyable day" on a 1–5 scale, with 1 being the worst and 5 the best. When assigning the rating, observers were told to think over the whole day and consider the frequency of student enthusiasm, boredom, overt inclusion, and exclusion. To anchor the ratings, observers participated in a weeklong training session prior to the summer in which they jointly watched videos and discussed ratings to resolve discrepancies. For more detail, see the online appendix.

with transition and mealtimes, positive teacher-student interactions also occurred throughout class time, during which teachers were friendly, engaged students in the content, and circulated among all students, not just some. Enrichment instructors actively facilitated and participated in such student activities as swimming or archery rather than watching on the side. Under the instruction of a participating, friendly adult, children displayed levels of engagement in such activities as crafts or dodge ball equal to what they displayed in novel activities, such as rock climbing, sailing, fencing, or tennis.

By contrast, on each day a RAND observer noted that students appeared to have a negative day (i.e., a 1 or 2 rating on the five-point scale from the daily site survey), we found that students experienced negative and often contradictory encounters, such as some adults saying an activity was prohibited while others allowed it. Examples of negative interactions include site staff being rude to or disengaged with students or providing poor student supervision, such as leaving the classroom for several minutes or allowing students to leave the class and wander. A negative atmosphere was often on display at mealtimes, when staff members yelled at students or required them to remain silent for the duration of the meal. We also observed teachers on their cell phones, reading magazines, and talking among themselves during class time while students completed low-effort activities, such as coloring or watching a video for long periods of time with no paired instruction.

Develop a Clear, Positive Message About the Summer Site Culture and Ask Staff to Convey It Consistently to Students

Consistency in behavior management and in value statements are key to a positive climate. Sites where students had outstanding days were almost all also rated as having consistent and appropriate behavioral management of students. Staff using similar words and concepts and engaging with students in similar (and often positive) behavior management was a sign of a coherent site culture. For example, staff might tell students "We don't do X here" or "At this site, we are about treating each other with kindness," indicating to observers that site leaders had communicated messages and expectations to staff prior to the summer session. Some sites used morning meetings and rituals to reinforce the goals and site culture to students and staff. In a few sites, these messages were explicitly tied to goals a site had for building social and emotional well-being for students. To support the development and communication of site culture, districts either provided goal statements or asked site leaders to create them (e.g., "Our activities are designed to encourage cooperation, communication, and taking initiative") and provided time for sites to have common training for their academic and enrichment staff.

Ensure Site Leaders Observe Instructional and Noninstructional Periods

Through frequent observations, site leaders can support teachers and ensure that staff are sending a consistent message about the site's values and behavioral expectations. Some summer site leaders routinely observed academic and enrichment instructors' summer classes, as well as transitions and lunch periods, while others rarely or never did so. In addition to class observations, being physically present during meals, arrival and departure, and the transition from academic to enrichment time is another important way site leaders can ensure consistent discipline and send staff and students an important message that they care about the program. By observing instructional and noninstructional periods, site leaders can understand whether the vision for site culture is being realized and can help support teachers and instructors who might be struggling.

If Resources Allow, Consider Hiring Staff to Support Positive Student Behavior

Bullying (and even fighting) can be a problem in summer programs in the same way that they are during the school year. For example, about half of summer program teachers in two of the five NSLP districts in summer 2013 reported that children were bullied and harassed by other students at least once a week. In one of these two districts, teachers reported bullying as a problem for three summers in a row. In response, the program leader decided to invest in two new positions for each site: social workers and behavioral management specialists. The social workers played many different roles. They established breakfast and lunch clubs in which small groups of (usually) girls ate together and proactively discussed relationship issues, facilitated by the social worker. They also visited families throughout the summer, particularly if a child was frequently absent. They purchased backup clothing, including bathing suits, to have on hand for the students and sent food home with students who appeared particularly hungry during the day. Before the summer program began, the behavior management specialists made a list of the students in their site who had been suspended during the school year. They then introduced themselves to these students and did "walkarounds"

> **TIP**
>
> Site leaders observing each instructor briefly at least once per week is a good way for leaders to identify which instructors are struggling and to ensure that staff are sending a consistent message to students in terms of behavior expectations and program values.

with them, during which they might play basketball or just talk to get to know each other better. They continued this relationship-building throughout the summer, expanding it to other children identified as struggling with behavior issues. At the end of the summer in which this district adopted the social work and behavioral management positions, surveyed teachers noted much less bullying (57 percent of teachers noted weekly bullying on the 2013 summer survey compared with 19 percent on the 2014 summer survey) and physical fighting (35 percent of teachers noted weekly physical fighting on the 2013 summer survey compared with 2 percent on the 2014 survey).

CHAPTER NINE

Program Costs and Revenues

Cost is of utmost concern to school districts in deciding whether and how widely to offer summer programming. The cost per student who attended at least one day of the summer 2014 program ranged from $1,070 to $1,700, with an average of $1,340. Districts can minimize costs—and maximize value from an investment in summer learning—by following these recommendations.

Cost is the largest barrier to districts offering summer programming to students. In summer 2014, we conducted a detailed examination of costs and revenues from three of the five NSLP districts that served multiple grade levels, which we presented in *Learning from Summer* (Augustine et al., 2016).

The cost per student who attended at least one day of the summer 2014 program ranged from $1,070 to $1,700 across the three districts offering programs at multiple grade levels. These numbers are shown in Table 9.1. The cost per filled seat—i.e., total cost divided by the average number of students present per day—ranged from $1,320 to $2,100, with an average of $1,860. These translate to an average hourly cost of $6.60 per student and $9.20 per filled seat.[5]

> The cost per student who attended at least one day of the summer 2014 program ranged from $1,070 to $1,700.

---

[5] Note that the summer programs have been in operation since at least 2010. As a result, the summer 2014 cost estimates reflected the cost of offering an ongoing summer program rather than launching a new program. In addition, we excluded the value of in-kind contributions (primarily in the form of staff time and the use of existing facilities) because we were unable to determine the reliability of districts' reporting of in-kind support.

TABLE 9.1

Per-Student Costs of 2014 Summer Programs Based on Three Programs Serving Multiple Grade Levels

Costs	Average	Low	High
Per student	$1,340.00	$1,070.00	$1,700.00
Per filled seat	$1,860.00	$1,320.00	$2,100.00
Per student per hour	$6.60	$5.70	$7.50
Per filled seat per hour	$9.20	$7.00	$12.40

SOURCE: Summer 2014 planning and execution cost data collected from three study districts.
NOTE: Cost per student is the cost per students who attended for at least one day. The cost per filled seat is the cost per students present, on average, each day.

As a point of reference, school-year costs in these districts ranged from $7.65 to $20.06 per student per hour, and 2013 national average school-year costs were $10.52 per student per hour (Cornman, 2015). These summer program cost estimates align with those from prior studies. Yeh (2017, p. 50) estimated summer program costs of $1,515 per attending student. In 2011, we found that the average costs from six district programs were $7 to $13 per student per hour and $8 to $19 per filled seat per hour (Augustine et al., 2013).

As during the school year, personnel commanded the largest share of expenditures in summer programs. Figure 9.1 shows the average expenditures for the 2014 summer learning programs in the three districts serving multiple grade levels.

Note that the three largest cost categories—academics, enrichment, and administrative—accounted for roughly 80 percent of total costs. Personnel was by far the largest driver of the overall costs of a program, making up the majority of total expenses, as the following list shows:

- Academic classroom staff salaries accounted for 35 percent of total expenditures, with district teacher salaries accounting for the vast majority of the costs in this category. Salaries for paraprofessionals, substitute teachers, and interns were also included, but made up only 4 percent of this category.

- District and site management, which accounted for 25 percent of total expenditures, consisted of central-office administrative positions, site-based program leaders, and non-teaching

FIGURE 9.1

2014 Average Summer Learning Program Expenditures in Three Districts

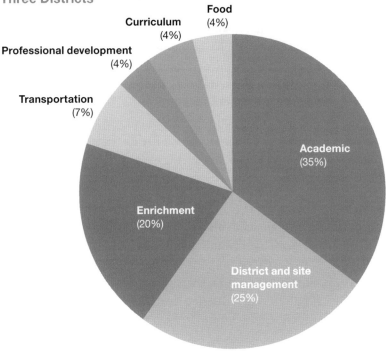

SOURCE: Augustine et al., 2016, p. 35.
NOTE: Numbers do not add to 100 percent due to rounding.

staff (such as guidance counselors and school administrative assistants).

- Enrichment was the third largest source of costs. This included field trips and district-employed music and physical education teachers. But the majority (85 percent) of enrichment costs was for contracted services with CBOs.

- Transportation, which accounted for 7 percent of total average expenditures, was primarily for daily busing but also included transportation to and from field trips.

- The curriculum category (4 percent) consisted of both district-level curriculum personnel (who helped select the curriculum and write pacing guides) and the ongoing costs to replace or update curriculum materials used in the classrooms.

- Professional development costs (4 percent) were primarily the cost of teachers' time for two to three days of professional development.

- Food accounted for an estimated 4 percent of total expenses, much of which was reimbursed through the federal meal program.

Programs were funded through a wide variety of funding portfolios. Sources consisted of private foundations, general funds from district budgets, Title I funding, and federal meal reimbursements. Across the districts, there were variations in the funding mix. Two of the five districts used little or no general district funds but did use Title I funding; the remaining three districts used general funds but not Title I. All five districts used federal meal reimbursements and, to varying extents, funding from private foundations.

The sources of revenue to support these programs have shifted over time, based on available funding. In 2011, these programs relied heavily on Title I funding, following an influx through the American Recovery and Reinvestment Act (Augustine et al., 2013). From 2011 to 2014, there was a significant reduction in Title I funding, which districts replaced with an increase in private foundation and general district funds.

Based on these analyses, we recommend several ways that districts can control costs while designing a program that meets students' needs.

Hire Staff to Achieve Desired Ratios Based on Projected Daily Attendance, Not the Initial Number of Enrollees

Not all students who sign up for summer programs actually attend them. Approximately two out of ten students who signed up did not attend the summer programs we studied. Those who did attend typically came about 75 percent of summer program days. During the planning phase, districts should refer to their historical no-show and attendance rates (or the averages presented in this guide if the district lacks historical data) to decide on numbers of staff needed for the summer program to reach desired adult-student ratios.

Approximately two out of ten students who signed up did not attend the summer programs we studied. Those who did attend typically came about 75 percent of summer program days.

Consider Cost-Efficiencies in the Design of the Program

Districts can lower the cost of summer programs in several ways. We present the main ones here. We note that some present trade-offs, and that program designers should weigh the savings from each against potential negative impacts on program quality.

Partner with Community-Based Organizations

Entering into partnerships with CBOs is one way to lower the cost of summer programs on a per-pupil basis. The NSLP full-day summer programs typically blended a half day of academic instruction with a half day of enrichment activities. The enrichment not only exposed students to activities they might not otherwise have had but also saved costs because enrichment staff typically earned lower wages. And in some cases, enrichment providers can use their own funding to cover summer program costs. In one district, enrichment providers funded their own services using their 21st Century Community Learning Centers funding. In two other districts, the fact that the summer program was offering a camp-like experience to low-income students attracted private businesses and local foundations to help support the enrichment costs.

Reduce the Number of Summer Facilities

Another cost-saving measure was to offer districtwide programs in as few buildings as possible (Augustine et al., 2013). It is more expensive to operate many small summer sites than it is to operate fewer larger summer sites because of fixed costs, such as full-time site leaders, meal delivery, and operating buildings during summer months. However, there also could be benefits to having smaller sites that outweigh these costs—e.g., an ability to host the program at a community facility with outdoor or other attractive learning opportunities for students, a shorter commute from home to site for more enrollees, or the ability to staff the summer site with home principals and teachers.

Centralize Planning Activities

Centralizing certain functions—such as transportation planning, curriculum design, professional development, and meal delivery—can help lower the costs of summer programs. It is more cost-efficient, for example, for a small, centralized team to develop a summer curriculum than to expect many different small summer sites to create their own.

Continue the Summer Program over Time to Reduce per-Pupil Costs

There are many up-front costs embedded in launching a summer program. In addition to curriculum design, there are costs associated with developing policies and procedures to select enrichment partners, developing recruitment materials and enrollment and attendance-taking processes, writing job descriptions, and planning professional development. These materials and procedures can be reused in subsequent summers, even if they need to be updated or improved. This helps lower per-pupil program costs by stretching the up-front investments over more summer program years.

Extend the School-Year Curricula

It is a significant up-front investment to develop or purchase summer curricula. One way to lower these costs would be having in-house district curriculum designers use the school-year curricula to develop additional lessons for a five- or six-week summer program. The organized collection and storage of summer instructional materials for their reuse in subsequent summers is another way to lower the costs of summer programs.

Abbreviations

CBO	community-based organization
ELA	English language arts
FRPL	free or reduced-price lunch
IEP	Individualized Education Program
NSLP	National Summer Learning Project

References

Alexander, Karl L., Doris R. Entwisle, and Linda S. Olson, "Schools, Achievement, and Inequality: A Seasonal Perspective," *Educational Evaluation and Policy Analysis*, Vol. 23, No. 2, 2001, pp. 171–191.

Atteberry, Allison, and Andrew McEachin, "School's Out: Summer Learning Loss Across Grade Levels and School Contexts in the U.S. Today," in Karl Alexander, Sarah Pitcock, and Matthew Boulay, eds., *The Summer Slide: What We Know and Can Do About Summer Learning Loss*, New York: Teachers College Press, 2016, pp. 35–54.

Augustine, Catherine H., Jennifer Sloan McCombs, John F. Pane, Heather L. Schwartz, Jonathan Schweig, Andrew McEachin, and Kyle Siler-Evans, *Learning from Summer: Effects of Voluntary Summer Learning Programs on Low-Income Urban Youth*, Santa Monica, Calif.: RAND Corporation, RR-1557-WF, 2016. As of January 19, 2018: https://www.rand.org/pubs/research_reports/RR1557.html

Augustine, Catherine H., Jennifer Sloan McCombs, Heather L. Schwartz, and Laura Zakaras, *Getting to Work on Summer Learning: Recommended Practices for Success*, Santa Monica, Calif.: RAND Corporation, RR-366-WF, 2013. As of January 19, 2018: https://www.rand.org/pubs/research_reports/RR366.html

Augustine, Catherine H., and Lindsey E. Thompson, *Making Summer Last: Integrating Summer Programming into Core District Priorities and Operations*, Santa Monica, Calif.: RAND Corporation, RR-2038-WF, 2017. As of January 19, 2018: https://www.rand.org/pubs/research_reports/RR2038.html

Chin, Tiffani, and Meredith Phillips, "Social Reproduction and Child-Rearing Practices: Social Class, Children's Agency, and the Summer Activity Gap," *Sociology of Education*, Vol. 77, No. 3, July 2004, pp. 185–210.

Cornman, Stephen Q., *Revenues and Expenditures for Public Elementary and Secondary Education: School Year 2012–13 (Fiscal Year 2013)*, Washington, D.C.: National Center for Education Statistics, U.S. Department of Education, NCES 2015-301, 2015. As of September 27, 2018:
https://nces.ed.gov/pubs2015/2015301.pdf

Downey, Douglas B., Paul von Hippel, and Beckett A. Broh, "Are Schools the Great Equalizer? Cognitive Inequality During the Summer Months and the School Year," *American Sociological Review*, Vol. 69, No. 5, 2004, pp. 613–635.

Durlak, Joseph A., and Emily P. DuPre, "Implementation Matters: A Review of Research on the Influence of Implementation on Program Outcomes and the Factors Affecting Implementation," *American Journal of Community Psychology*, Vol. 41, 2008, pp. 327–350.

Fisher, Charles W., David C. Berliner, Nikola N. Filby, Richard Marliave, Leonard S. Cahen, and Marilyn M. Dishaw, "Teaching Behaviors, Academic Learning Time, and Student Achievement: An Overview," in Carolyn Denham and Ann Lieberman, eds., *Time to Learn: A Review of the Beginning Teacher Evaluation Study*, Sacramento, Calif.: California State Commission for Teacher Preparation and Licensing, 1980, pp. 7–32.

Harnischfeger, Annegret, and David E. Wiley, "The Teaching-Learning Process in Elementary Schools: A Synoptic View," *Curriculum Inquiry*, Vol. 6, No. 1, 1976, pp. 5–43.

Hawley, Willis D., Susan Rosenholtz, Henry J. Goodstein, and Ted Hasselbring, "Good Schools: What Research Says About Improving Student Achievement," *Peabody Journal of Education*, Vol. 61, No. 4, 1984, pp. iii–178.

Karweit, Nancy, "Should We Lengthen the School Year?" *Educational Researcher*, Vol. 14, No. 6, 1985, pp. 9–15.

Karweit, Nancy, and Robert E. Slavin, "Time-on-Task: Issues of Timing, Sampling, and Definition," *Journal of Education Psychology*, Vol. 74, No. 6, 1982, pp. 844–851.

Lomax, Richard G., and William W. Cooley, "The Student Achievement-Instructional Time Relationship," paper presented at the Annual Meeting of the American Educational Research Association, San Francisco, Calif., April 1979.

Martorell, Paco, Trey Miller, Lucrecia Santibañez, and Catherine H. Augustine, "Can Incentives for Parents and Students Change Educational Inputs? Experimental Evidence from Summer School," *Economics of Education Review*, Vol. 50, February 2016, pp. 113–126.

McCombs, Jennifer Sloan, Catherine H. Augustine, Heather L. Schwartz, Susan J. Bodilly, Brian McInnis, Dahlia S. Lichter, and Amanda Brown Cross, *Making Summer Count: How Summer Programs Can Boost Children's Learning*, Santa Monica, Calif.: RAND Corporation, MG-1120-WF, 2011. As of September 24, 2018:
http://www.rand.org/pubs/monographs/MG1120.html

McCombs, Jennifer Sloan, John F. Pane, Catherine H. Augustine, Heather L. Schwartz, Paco Martorell, and Laura Zakaras, *Ready for Fall? Near-Term Effects of Voluntary Summer Learning Programs on Low-Income Students' Learning Opportunities and Outcomes*, Santa Monica, Calif.: RAND Corporation, RR-815-WF, 2014. As of January 22, 2018:
https://www.rand.org/pubs/research_reports/RR815.html

National School Climate Center, "Our Approach," webpage, undated. As of January 19, 2018:
http://www.schoolclimate.org/climate/

Penuel, William R., Barry J. Fishman, Ryoko Yamaguchi, and Lawrence P. Gallagher, "What Makes Professional Development Effective? Strategies That Foster Curriculum Implementation," *American Educational Research Journal*, Vol. 44, No. 4, 2007, pp. 921–958.

Rivkin, Steven G., Eric A. Hanushek, and John F. Kain, "Teachers, Schools, and Academic Achievement," *Econometrica*, Vol. 73, No. 2, 2005, pp. 417–458.

Rowan, Brian, Richard Correnti, and Robert J. Miller, "What Large-Scale Research Tells Us About Teacher Effects on Student Achievement: Insights from the Prospects Study of Elementary Schools," *Teachers College Record*, Vol. 104, No. 8, 2002, pp. 1525–1567.

Sanders, William L., and Sandra P. Horn, "Research Findings from the Tennessee Value-Added Assessment System (TVAAS) Database: Implications for Educational Evaluation and Research," *Journal of Personnel Evaluation in Education*, Vol. 12, No. 3, 1998, pp. 247–256.

Sanders, William L., and June C. Rivers, *Research Progress Report: Cumulative and Residual Effects of Teachers on Future Student Academic Achievement: Tennessee Value-Added System*, Knoxville, Tenn.: University of Tennessee Value-Added Research and Assessment Center, 1996.

The Wallace Foundation, Summer Learning Toolkit, assorted webpages, undated. As of November 2018: http://www.summerlearningtoolkit.org

Wimer, Christopher, Susanne M. Bouffard, Pia Caronongan, Eric Dearing, Sandra Simpkins, Priscilla Little, and Heather Weiss, *What Are Kids Getting into These Days? Demographic Differences in Youth Out-of-School Time Participation*, Cambridge, Mass.: Harvard Family Research Project, 2006. As of September 27, 2018: https://eric.ed.gov/?id=ED491181

Wright, S. Paul, Sandra P. Horn, and William L. Sanders, "Teacher and Classroom Context Effects on Student Achievement: Implications for Teacher Evaluation," *Journal of Personnel Evaluation in Education*, Vol. 11, 1997, pp. 57–67.

Yeh, Stuart S., *Solving the Achievement Gap: Overcoming the Structure of School Inequality*, New York: Springer, 2017.

Appendix Materials

Getting to Work
on **Summer Learning**

Recommended Practices
for Success, 2nd Ed.

Heather L. Schwartz, Jennifer Sloan McCombs,
Catherine H. Augustine, Jennifer T. Leschitz

Commissioned by

The Wallace Foundation

Supporting ideas.
Sharing solutions.
Expanding opportunities.

For more information on this publication, visit www.rand.org/t/RR366-1

Published by the RAND Corporation, Santa Monica, Calif.
© Copyright 2018 RAND Corporation
RAND® is a registered trademark.

Support RAND
Make a tax-deductible charitable contribution at
www.rand.org/giving/contribute

www.rand.org

Preface

This appendix augments a report that updates our 2013 guidance to school district leaders and their partners across the country who are interested in launching summer learning programs or improving established ones. In that report, we present recommendations based on our evaluations, conducted between 2011 and 2016, of summer programs in five urban school districts. The Wallace Foundation selected these districts—Boston; Dallas; Duval County, Florida; Pittsburgh; and Rochester, New York—for the National Summer Learning Project (NSLP), a multiyear assessment of the effectiveness of voluntary, district-led summer learning programs offered at no cost to low-income, urban, elementary students. The five districts are among the nation's most advanced in their experience with comprehensive, voluntary summer learning programs.

This study was undertaken by RAND Education and Labor, a division of the RAND Corporation that conducts research on early childhood through postsecondary education programs, workforce development, and programs and policies affecting workers, entrepreneurship, and financial literacy and decisionmaking. This study was sponsored by The Wallace Foundation, which seeks to support and share effective ideas and practices to improve learning and enrichment for disadvantaged children and the vitality of the arts for everyone. Its current objectives are to improve the quality of schools, primarily by developing and placing effective principals in high-need schools; promoting social and emotional learning in elementary school and out-of-school-time settings; reimagining and expanding learning time during the traditional school day and year, as well as during the summer months; expanding access to arts learning; and developing audiences for the arts. For more information and research on these and other related topics, please visit its Knowledge Center at www.wallacefoundation.org.

More information about RAND can be found at www.rand.org. Questions about this report should be directed to Heather Schwartz at heather_schwartz@rand.org, and questions about RAND Education and Labor should be directed to educationandlabor@rand.org.

Contents

Tables

1. Collection of Primary Data

In summers 2011–2014, we collected primary data about the implementation of the summer programs in the five National Summer Learning Project (NSLP) school districts. These included surveys, interviews, and summer site observations in each of the four summers, as shown in Table A.1.

Table A.1. Primary Data Collected for the NSLP Study

Summer	Interviews of Summer Program Staff	Surveys of Summer Instructors	Surveys of Parents	Surveys and Tests of Students	Hours of Observation of Summer Classes	Ratings Completed at End of Observation Day	Reviews of Summer Curricula
2011	325	293	817	631	216	0	6
2012	256	560	101	0	300	0	10
2013	218	192	0	5,134	783	0	0
2014	113	173	0	4,525	760	147	0
Total	912	1,218	918	10,290	2,059	147	16

SOURCE: RAND formative feedback reports to NSLP districts.
NOTE: RAND researchers collected all these data, except for (1) student surveys and tests, which Mathematica administered in the fall 2013 and fall 2014, and (2) the review of the summer 2012 curricula, which was conducted by curricular consultants.

Throughout this second edition of the guide, we cite findings from our prior reports in the summer series, including *Getting to Work on Summer Learning* (about summer 2011 implementation),[1] *Ready for Fall?* (about summer 2013 implementation and outcomes),[2] *Learning from Summer* (about summers 2013 and 2014 implementation and outcomes),[3] and *Making Summer Last* (about sustaining summer programs by integrating them into core district activities).[4] Each of these reports contains the relevant technical information explaining the analyses underlying their findings and recommendations. In this appendix, we describe the two

---

[1] Catherine H. Augustine, Jennifer Sloan McCombs, Heather L. Schwartz, and Laura Zakaras, *Getting to Work on Summer Learning: Recommended Practices for Success*, Santa Monica, Calif.: RAND Corporation, RR-366-WF, 2013. As of January 19, 2018: https://www.rand.org/pubs/research_reports/RR366.html

[2] Jennifer Sloan McCombs, John F. Pane, Catherine H. Augustine, Heather L. Schwartz, Paco Martorell, and Laura Zakaras, *Ready for Fall? Near-Term Effects of Voluntary Summer Learning Programs on Low-Income Students' Learning Opportunities and Outcomes*, Santa Monica, Calif.: RAND Corporation, RR-815-WF, 2014. As of January 22, 2018: https://www.rand.org/pubs/research_reports/RR815.html

[3] Catherine H. Augustine, Jennifer Sloan McCombs, John F. Pane, Heather L. Schwartz, Jonathan Schweig, Andrew McEachin, and Kyle Siler-Evans, *Learning from Summer: Effects of Voluntary Summer Learning Programs on Low-Income Urban Youth*, Santa Monica, Calif.: RAND Corporation, RR-1557-WF, 2016. As of January 19, 2018: https://www.rand.org/pubs/research_reports/RR1557.html

[4] Catherine H. Augustine and Lindsey E. Thompson, *Making Summer Last: Integrating Summer Programming into Core District Priorities and Operations*, Santa Monica, Calif.: RAND Corporation, RR-2038-WF, 2017. As of January 19, 2018: https://www.rand.org/pubs/research_reports/RR2038.html

sources of data for the new analyses performed for this updated edition of the guide: classroom observations from summer 2014 and daily site climate surveys from summer 2014.

Summer Site Observations

In summer 2014, trained RAND observers conducted at least two daylong observations in each of 32 total summer sites in the five NSLP districts. These observers spent one program day from bus arrival to bus departure following a single student cohort. All of these summer students were fourth-graders rising into fifth grade, and all were attending summer programs that were voluntary and had the common characteristics of The Wallace Foundation's demonstration (e.g., full-day programs of five to six weeks in length).

The number of days that observers spent at each summer site depended on the number of student cohorts served. For example, if a site had four classes of fourth-graders (e.g., green, red, yellow, and orange rooms), observers spent four days at the site—one day to follow the green room, the second to observe the red room, and so on. In the rare instance of a site having only one classroom cohort, RAND observers spent two days with the same cohort to better represent site activities. Observers noted as few as 10 percent to as many as 40 percent of the program days at any given site. Thus, the site observations do not necessarily characterize each site's entire summer program.

To the degree possible, RAND observers were on site during the second week of the five- or six-week program to avoid observing start-up days; they did not observe field trip days when classes were typically suspended; and they avoided any observations during the last two or three days of the summer program because these were often wind-down days or culminating activity days when activities did not proceed as normal. RAND observers also sought to stagger site visits evenly across the days of the week and the weeks of the summer session. For example, an observer would arrange his or her schedule to observe as many sites as possible for one day during week two, one day during week three, etc., and that observer purposely scheduled visits to occur on different days of the week so that a given site was not always observed on a Monday or a Friday.

Table A.2 shows the number and distribution of daylong observations in summer 2014.

Table A.2. Total Observation Days by District in Summer 2014

District	Total Number of RAND Observation Days	Number of Summer Sites
Boston	33	10
Dallas	35	8
Duval	34	8
Pittsburgh	13	3
Rochester	32	1, organized into 3 "houses"
Total	**147**	**32**

Observers arrived slightly before students did so that they could watch the arrival process and transitions to breakfast and then class. They then watched the rest of the classroom cohort's day through mathematics, English language arts (ELA), and enrichment instruction until departure. The aim was to see the "in-between" moments, as well as all class time, to gain a student-centered view of the experience of a summer program day.

We developed our own classroom observation protocol in 2011 designed specifically to measure certain key aspects of our theoretical framework about how summer programs might lead to gains in student learning. This protocol gathered information on the quality of instruction; time on task; and other aspects of the classroom, such as warmth and climate. We further refined the protocol for summers 2013 and 2014. The summer 2014 protocol is provided at the end of this appendix. To measure time on task, RAND observers attended and coded the entire class, whether it was 30 or 120 minutes, to capture the amount of intended time spent on instruction.

Table A.3 shows the number of observations we conducted by subject. We excluded such subjects as science, SuccessMaker, Walk to Intervention, and social studies, which were offered by some districts but were not universal. The number of enrichment observations exceeds mathematics and ELA observations because many sites offered more than one enrichment session per day for students (e.g., archery taught by an archery instructor and then swimming by a swimming instructor).

Table A.3. Total Classroom Observations by Subject in Summer 2014

Subject	Number of Observations
ELA	136
Mathematics	127
Enrichment	179

NOTE: All observations of these subjects were conducted during 147 total summer observation days.

3

Definition of Instructional and Noninstructional Time

In Chapter Four of the main report, we present statistics on the percentage of intended instructional minutes lost to noninstructional time. These statistics derive from the time log portion of the class observation tool. To complete the time log, we coded each class segment (e.g., whole-group instruction, guided practice, independent practice, and noninstructional times) and provided qualitative descriptions of the activity during that segment. If a majority of students during an instructional activity became visibly off task (e.g., sleeping, walking around, talking to friends), the RAND observer then started a new time log entry coded as "NI" for noninstructional and described what was happening during this time. Active class time during which there was no instruction (e.g., students filing into the room, teacher collecting papers, or teacher stopping instruction to discipline a student) was also coded as "NI." An event had to last for at least one full minute for a RAND observer to create a new entry in the time log. Time log entries about instructional and noninstructional time are the data source for the discussions of afternoon slump, independent practice time, and time use in ELA classes.

Definition of Outstanding, Good, Mixed, or Poor Classes

The rating variable could take one of four values: outstanding, good, mixed, or poor. Trained RAND observers assigned this global rating at the end of the completed class observation, taking into consideration productive use of class time, factual accuracy of instruction, teachers' checking for student understanding, and whether the teacher was engaged or disengaged (e.g., checking his or her phone or leaving the room).

Definition of Outstanding, Good, Mixed, or Poor Days

To characterize an entire summer program day, we combined data elements from the two sources of data. We first restricted our definition of "entire summer program day" to one in which we observed all of the following: at least one mathematics class, at least one ELA class, and at least one enrichment class. Out of our 147 summer observation days, 123 of them (84 percent) met this definition. Although school districts expected that all three types of classes generally would occur daily, there were sometimes deviations from this plan for any of the following reasons: The day a RAND observer was scheduled to follow a class turned out to be a field trip day, in which case he or she observed the field trip; weather caused the last-minute cancellation of outdoor classes; or sites ran computer courses that day in lieu of a mathematics or ELA class.

We categorized the 123 observation days that met our criteria into four tiers. "Outstanding" days were those in which RAND observers rated all of the academic and enrichment class observations on that day as either "good" or "outstanding" and rated on the end-of-day survey that students appeared to enjoy the day. "Good" days were those in which the RAND observer rated at least one of the mathematics, ELA, or enrichment classes as "good" or "outstanding" and none of the observed classes as "terrible," and they rated on the end-of-day survey that students appeared to enjoy the day. On a "mixed" day, the RAND observer rated students' enjoyment of the day as a 3 on the five-point end-of-day survey scale, with no stipulations about mathematics, ELA, or enrichment classroom ratings. Finally, on a "negative" day, the RAND observer rated students' enjoyment of the day as a 1 or a 2 on the five-point end-of-day survey scale, with no stipulations about mathematics, ELA, or enrichment classroom ratings.

Daily Site Climate Surveys

To characterize each summer site's climate, we analyzed survey data that RAND observers completed at the end of the observation days as we have described. The end-of-day survey form is included at the end of this appendix. One item in particular is central for the analysis in this guide: the observer's rating of 1 (worst) to 5 (best) on the item "Students appeared to have enjoyable day." The observers were trained to use the survey instrument during a weeklong training in spring 2014. When assigning the rating, observers were told to think over the whole day and consider the frequency of student enthusiasm, boredom, overt inclusion, and exclusion. To anchor the ratings, observers jointly rated videos in training sessions prior to the summer and discussed ratings to resolve discrepancies. Specifically, each observer attended a three-day in-person training that involved watching videos, rating them, and discussing the ratings. Each observer reached agreement with at least 85 percent of the preratings done by the two trainers of each video.

2. Documentation Used in Classroom Observations

2014 Classroom Observation Protocol

Overview

		Observation ID:	19000100

		Input
1	OBSERVER. Observer initials:	
2	DATE. Date [MM/DD/YYYY]:	
3	CITYID. [Boston=B; Dallas=D; Jacksonville=J; Pittsburgh=P; Rochester=R]	
4	SITEID. School/site Identifier [S1, S2, etc.]:	
5	TEACHID. Teacher Identifier [T1, T2, etc.]. Use ENR1, ENR2, ENR3 for 1st, 2nd, 3rd, etc. RAND observed enr session of the day:	
6	TEACHSUB. Indicate if substitute teacher [N/Y]:	
7	RANDCOHORT. Student cohort group identifier [C1, C2, C3, etc.]. Skip if ENR or WTI.	
8	TEACHNAMELAST. Write last name of teacher and confirm correct Teacher ID above.	
9	DISTRICTCOHORT. Write the district language to identify the group and confirm correct RAND Cohort ID.	
10	SCHEDBEGIN. Class period scheduled beginning [HH:MM]:	
11	BEGINOTHER. Main reason, if any, for class starting at a different time:	
12	SCHEDEND. Class period scheduled ending [HH:MM] [AM/PM]:	
13	ENDOTHER. Main reason, if any, for class ending at a different time:	
14	SUBJECT. Subject of class: [M for math, ELA, ENR for enrichment, SCI for science, SS for social studies, IR for iReady, ELA-R for Writing, ELA-B for bilingual language arts]	
15	NUMSTUD_START. Number of students (start):	
16	NUMSTUD_END. Number of students (end):	
17	SPANISH. Choose Y/N if any instruction including clarification occurred in Spanish in this class.	

Academic Class Segments

Time begin	Description (I, NI, or End)	NI sub-codes	Teacher modeled what students will do (I do)	Whole-group guided practice (We do)	Small-group instruction (We do; teacher or para are delivering instruction to students)	Independent practice (You do)	Duration	Summarize the major activity of the segment & positive or negative aspects of the segment

18) RUNNING TIME LOG. See comments below for directions. Remember to always end your log with "END" to indicate the end of class.

Directions: Start a new row for each new activity. Segments are at least 60 seconds long. Your time log should begin when a majority of students are in the room, regardless of whether the teacher has launched the lesson. The log should end when the majority of students leave the room. You should watch and record the entire class period.

Time begin:
Time of the start of the class and subsequent class segments is needed to calculate actual time, time on and off task, and time of independent practice. Start a new row for each new activity. Segments must be at least 60 seconds long to initiate new row. Your time log should begin when a majority of students are in the room, regardless of whether the teacher has launched the lesson.

Description:
I indicates that majority of students are engaged in an instructional activity.
NI indicates a majority of students not engaged in an subject-related instructional activity for more than 60 seconds, e.g., off-topic conversation, class started late or ended early, transition to the next activity, teacher involved in management activities, break in class.
End indicates the end of the class period.

Sub-codes for noninstruction:
Teacher sets out classroom/behavior rules (R) includes activities such as teacher explaining what good behavior means in this classroom and what she expects. It does not include "get in a line" or disciplinary time, which should be coded as T.
Teacher-initiated interruption (T) includes administrative activities such as teacher taking attendance, passing out materials, or moving desks; transitions between class activities; teacher addressing behavior; bathroom breaks; and snack breaks.
Externally initiated interruption (E) includes principal visit or loudspeaker announcement that stops teaching, fire drill, or other unscheduled interruption out of teacher's control.
Pause for scheduled break in class **(P)**, for example, lunch and recess occur between part 1 and 2 of an ELA lesson. This code allows us to pause the class segments timer.

Teacher modeled what students will do (I do): Teacher explicitly models what students will do. The teacher is delivering direct instruction that builds students' understanding of ELA or mathematics. Teacher models step by step how students will do an academic task; there is little to no student participation during the teacher modeling.

Whole-group guided practice (We do): "Yes" indicates that the teacher facilitates in a structured or semistructured way a whole-group activity where the kids demonstrate or practice a skill as a whole group. Some students might practice or demonstrate a skill or strategy in front of the entire class, share their thinking about how or why they used the skill or strategy, and received feedback. Although only some students may answers or solutions aloud, all students have an opportunity to hear how to practice the targeted skill or strategy. All students might complete portions of an activity before reviewing the concepts as a class. *Guided practice sets students up to successfully complete an application activity of the skill or strategy independently. Guided practice provides teachers an opportunity to understand if students have a misconception and where the misconception or misunderstanding may be occurring.* I-R-E that asks only for the correct answer and does not require students to share their thinking or approach to completing the activity is not guided practice. A student who doesn't understand a concept would benefit from seeing guided practice. Teacher question: What is the vocabulary word that means low cost? Student response: Inexpensive. What is 3+5? Or what is the solution to number 5? does not count as guided practice. Reviewing solutions or answers without conceptual discussion does not count as guided practice.

Example of whole-group guided practice in mathematics: What is the first step to solving the problem? How do you know? Is there another way we would have started this problem? What do we do next? Teacher facilitates a discussion where students solve a fraction equation aloud is an example of whole-group guided practice. All students might write the steps on worksheets while they solve the problem or steps might be written on the board as a reference for students.

Example of whole-group guided practice in ELA: Teacher reads a passage aloud and asks students to summarize the passage. Student shares summary and teacher asks questions of other students about why details were excluded from the summary and others were included in the summary. Asks students for other variations of the summary. Teacher may distribute four different passages to students. Asks students to develop a summary for the passage as a team, present the summary, and explain rationale for what was included or excluded in the summary. As the independent practice, students would summarize passages in their independent reading books or a worksheet for a sustained period of time. In a mini-lesson, students may be asked to edit the passage from the teacher's writer's notebook. Students and teachers provide feedback and discuss editing choices before students edit text passages independently.

Small-group guided practice (We do): "Yes" indicates that the teacher facilitates in a structured or semistructured way an activity that provides insights into the existence of misconceptions in students and where the misconception or misunderstanding may occur. Guided practice sets the small group of students up to successfully complete an application activity of the skill or strategy independently. The teacher could also reteach a mini-lesson to a small group of students if the teacher determines only a group experiences a misconception or misunderstanding that prevents successful independent practice.

Independent practice (You do): "Yes" indicates that students have independent practice opportunity with subject content for that time segment
Independent Practice (YES if it occurs): Students have independent practice, whether in small groups or independent work. Do not count pair-and-shares or brief (< 2 min) activities. Students completes activities without consistent support from the teacher (e.g., reading a book and filling out a worksheet).

Duration:
Minute value is automatically calculated by the time entries.

Summary:
In this cell, the observer summarizes the content, structure, and characteristics (what is the teacher doing, what are the kids doing) of that time segment for both I and NI. It is important to clearly describe what is happening during instances of active teacher instruction, guided practice, independent practice, and discussion of text.

Enrichment Class Segments

Time begin	Description (I, NI, or End)	NI sub-codes	If activity, are the majority of students participating?	Duration	Summarize the major activity of the segment & positive or negative aspects of the segment

19) RUNNING TIME LOG. <u>See comments below for directions</u>. Remember to always end your log with "END" to indicate the end of class.

Directions: When kids start an activity on their own or do an activity, start a new segment.

Evidence of Classroom Practices

		Yes/No
20)	**Evidence of classroom practices.** *For each statement below, enter "Y" if you see the practice, and "N" if you did not see the practice or if it does not apply. Skip this table if you are observing a class with no intended instruction—e.g., recess, only independent reading, only independent writing, or iReady in Duval.*	
a.	STATE_GOAL. Prior to students doing independent practice, the teacher explained or wrote down what students would do or what skills they would cover during the overall session.	
b.	STATE_PURPOSE. The teacher states the purpose for what they will do—i.e., why students would learn the skill in terms of real-world relevance. Math example: T: "Why is area important? It helps us to know how much tile to order if I'm retiling my kitchen floor." Lowest threshold of acceptable ELA example: Before students begin indep practice about reading about inferences, T: "Good readers infer things from clues in the text." Stronger ELA example: T: "You are all authors, and as authors, you want to give your readers clues to help readers infer traits about your characters."	
c.	ONTASK. This class is characterized as focused and attentive students. Large majority of students are on task throughout class period. Students are focused and attentive to the task/ project. They follow along with the staff and/or follow directions to carry on an individual or group task. Noise level and youth interactions can be high if youth are engaged in the expected task(s). Mark no if more than 10% students are off task for 1 or more full segment of the class.	
d.	CHECK_UNDERSTANDING. Teacher **BOTH** (1) performs ongoing assessment throughout the whole class period by checking for students' understanding of content, and (2) addresses misunderstandings if and as they arise through new instruction (not just "look at that again"). T takes the students' temperature via Qs, pop quizzes, popsicle sticks, or other ways like indep work, then T verifies whether all students understand and seems to *adjust instruction based on students' understanding. By end of class period, you think T knows each student's level of understanding, but* **does NOT require** *that all students understand the concept by the end of class.* For enrichment, T's visual assessment of student performance is sufficient.	
e.	ENTHUSIASM. All or almost all students exhibited obvious signs of enthusiasm for the class throughout the class period (e.g., jumping out of seat, quickly & enthusiastically answering teacher's questions). If almost all students enthusiastic, but more than one student is checked out throughout the whole class period, rate no. For enrichment, all or almost all kids are having fun in intended activity.	
f.	CONTENT. The teacher exhibited obvious signs of enthusiasm about the content of the class (e.g., conveys that the content is important to understand, exuberant affect about the material, good explanations about why students are doing the material or reflects deep knowledge of content, T gets excited about or helps students make connections, brings in additional materials to extend the content of the lesson).	
g.	INACCURATE. The teacher provided or failed to correct factually inaccurate information that would confuse students about the content/skills they were to learn. If there are multiple minor mistakes that relate to the skills/content taught, rate as yes. (Do not count minor mistakes that do not relate to the skills being taught—e.g., stating "today is Tuesday" when it is Wednesday.)	
h.	UNCLEAR. Teacher's explanation of the instructional content was unclear, hard to follow, incomplete, or inconsistent. Mark no if all or almost all students clearly know what to do throughout the class. Mark yes if teacher's instruction is clear even if students struggle in independent practice to complete the task. Use this to distinguish poor teachers from fair/good teachers.	

i.	INTERRUPT. When the teacher disciplined students, the majority of the class was either interrupted for a long period (2+ minutes) or a series of short interruptions that are nitpicking, unnecessary interruptions (about sitting up straight, hands folded, holding pencils correctly). *If there are no instances of students misbehavior, mark no.*	
j.	WELL_OILED. Focus on mechanics instead of instructional content. Little to no time is wasted; pacing is efficient. Kids know what to do procedurally throughout the class. The flow and mechanics of the class are smooth, not choppy. Plus, procedures are in place & material available to occupy children productively throughout the class (e.g., differentiated materials during independent practice). During each activity, kids knew what to do and a majority were on task. The class resembles a "well-oiled machine" where a majority of students know what is expected of them and how to go about doing it throughout the whole class.	
k.	RIGOR. Lesson is characterized by appropriately challenging, rigorous tasks that engage critical thinking skills. For example: Teacher asks questions that get students to get at the "why." Students use multiple ways to solve a problem that expands their conceptual knowledge of mathematics. Students engage in meaningful discussion of text. Only rate yes for rigor in ELA if students are engaged in meaningful discussion of text. Students appear to be appropriately challenged. If it seems like busywork, do not code lesson as rigorous. NA for enrichment.	
l.	HELPFUL_ADULTS. There was a helpful adult other than the teacher in the classroom. Helpful means the adult either worked directly with students or helped the teacher in some way (handing out worksheets; working with an IEP student; helping with classroom management). Rate NA if there was not another adult in the classroom.	

Evidence of Summer School Climate

21) Evidence of summer school climate. *For each statement below, enter "y" if you see the practice, and "n" if you did not see the practice or if it does not apply. Skip this table if you are observing a class with no intended instruction—e.g., recess, only independent reading, only independent writing, or iReady in Duval.*

		Yes/No
a.	RESPECT. Students respect one another. They refrain from derogatory comments or actions about an individual person and the work s/he is doing; if disagreements occur, they are handled constructively.	
b.	FRIENDLY. Students verbally encourage each other, are overtly friendly and supportive.	
c.	LIKE_TEACHER. Students show explicit signs that they have warm, positive affect to teacher (not just respect for teachers). For example, throughout the class they may smile at teacher, laugh with them, and/or share good-natured jokes.	
d.	LIKE_STUDENTS. Teacher shows explicit signs of caring and positive affect toward youth. Mark no if teacher is simply respectful toward students. Teacher tone is warm and caring. He or she uses positive language, smiles, laughs, or shares good-natured jokes throughout class. If no verbal interaction is necessary, teacher demonstrates a positive and caring affect toward youth. *If you were a student in this class, you would think the teacher cared about you.*	
e.	DISRESPECTFUL. In at least one instance, the teacher was disrespectful to students. This includes yelling at one or more students, intimidating or being rude or dismissive to students, using physical aggression, intentionally humiliating or ignoring a student, using discriminatory acts or derogatory language to students.	
f.	MISBEHAVIOR. There was one or more flagrant instance of student misbehavior. This includes a physical fight or persistent bullying or persistent use of discriminatory or derogatory language.	
g.	PERSIST. The teacher (a) explicitly encouraged at least one student struggling with a particular tasks to persist at academic/content-related tasks that were difficult for them (e.g., exhortations to keep trying, you know you can do it, helping students stick with rather than quit a task, to stretch to a higher level than the one student currently performs at), or (b) explicitly taught students strategies to persist at tasks.	
h.	SOCIALSKILLS. The teacher *explicitly* taught social skills, such as respecting, listening, cooperating with, or helping others or teaching of politeness. Do not check if these skills were implicitly involved.	
i.	TDISENGAGED. The teacher responsible for the activity was disengaged in the classroom because of an apathetic, flat affect, by going through the motions, or exerting extremely low effort (e.g., reading off script without deviation) or because of distractions by factors that were within his/her control (i.e., a teacher stopping by to have a conversation about the weekend, the teacher checking his/her cell phone, texting, or taking or making a personal call that was not related to an emergency, personal chat with co-teacher or paraprofessional while students are working).	
J.	BORED. All or almost all students in the class appeared bored throughout the class. Boredom characterized the class period, even if students complied with teachers' requests. NA for academics.	

Overall Reactions

OVERALL REACTIONS. Type in white cells below your overall impressions. Row height will expand as you type.		
22)	INSTRUCT_CONTENT. Choose Y/N if there was any academic content covered in the intended subject. Enrichment is NA.	▾
23)	LEARNED. Based on evidence of student demonstrations, what did students learn?	
24)	BARRIERS. What, if any, were the main impediments or barriers to learning in this class? Note, please give examples of factual inaccuracies or shortage of materials.	
25)	TEXTS. For ELA classes only: how much text did the majority of students read indivdually in this class? Exclude teacher oral reading, round robin, overheads. Rate NA for non-ELA classes.	
26)	TEXT_COMMENT. For ELA only: Characterize amount of text that negative and positive outliers read and indicate how prevalent these outliers were in class. Type NA if not ELA.	
27)	RATING. Rate this class terrible, mixed, good, or outstanding.	
28)	RATING_JUSTIFY. In a few words, justify your rating.	

End-of-Day Site Survey

Please complete the daily survey each day. The daily survey is intended to capture your overall experiences at a site each day of the summer program.

The survey requires a response to every item. It is not possible to submit the survey if there is a blank text box or missing rating on the scales. There is a note above each text box that lists the range of accepted responses: yes, no, or NA. For example, "no" is an acceptable response to questions about data collection.

1. Date of observation

    mm/dd/yyyy

    [   ]

2. Site observed

    [-- Please Select --   ▾]

3. Observer's initials

    [   ]

4. Are there any questions from site staff that a RAND leader needs to follow up on?

   If no questions, enter no. If questions, type the question(s) that require a response and indicate to whom the response should be directed.

5. List data collection activities completed; specifically, the site, teacher, cohort, subject of the group(s) of students you observed, and if interview(s) conducted. List the site and name of interviewee.

   If you were able to complete activities as planned, begin response with "as planned."

   If you were unable to complete an activity as planned, explicitly state what was not accomplished and, if appropriate, the change made in the field.

   A substitute teacher is an example of a change in the field. Please note if there was a substitute present and if the observation was completed with a substitute.

6. Any questions about data collection (e.g., how to complete protocol based on observation)?

   If no questions, enter no.

7. Any problems or issues with logistics observed (transportation, materials, supplies, poor attendance taking, AC, lack of space)?

   If no logistical problems observed, enter no.

14

8. Were there any notable observations regarding non-classroom time (i.e. breakfast, lunch, recess, snack, morning meeting, hallway transitions; positive and negative actions of staff and students applies here)?

If no positive or negative observations, enter no. If positive but no negative, describe the positive observations and state no negative observations. If negative but no positive, describe the negative observations and state no positive observations.

9. Alarming events (fight, shootings, thefts, drug sales, loitering, kids getting lost, bullying)?

If no alarming events, enter no.

10. Were there any comments from adults at the site about program quality?

If a comment was OFF THE RECORD, please note OTR in front of comment to ensure the comment remains internal to the research team. If no program quality comments, enter no.

11. What is the best thing that you observed today? Provide evidence, could be instructional.

If there was not a best thing observed, enter NA.

12. What is the worst thing that you observed today? Provide evidence, could be instructional.

If there was not a worst thing observed, enter NA.

13. Based on your experience and observation of 4go5 students TODAY, rate the following site-level dimensions (not specific to individual classes or actors):

When answering these questions, think specifically about today's observations of 4go5 students.

	1	2	3	4	5	
Adults at the site do not address student behavior consistently or appropriately	☐	☐	☐	☐	☐	Adults at the site address student behavior consistently and appropriately when misbehavior occurs
Student misbehavior is common at this site	☐	☐	☐	☐	☐	Almost none or no student misbehavior at this site
Site is chaotic (no routines, unorganized transitions, poor communication among staff)	☐	☐	☐	☐	☐	Site is well-organized (predictable routines, smooth transitions, clear communication among staff)
Students appeared to have terrible day	☐	☐	☐	☐	☐	Students appeared to have enjoyable day
Staff are hostile toward students	☐	☐	☐	☐	☐	Staff are overtly friendly toward students
Multiple instances of students being mean to one another	☐	☐	☐	☐	☐	Students are overtly friendly toward and supportive of one another

14. Please describe here any additional comments about the atmosphere and culture of the site observed today that have not been captured above.

If no additional comments, enter no.